THE DEVIL'S DEFENDER

THE DEVIL'S DEFENDER

My Odyssey Through American Criminal Justice from Ted Bundy to the Kandahar Massacre

JOHN HENRY BROWNE

Published by Chicago Review Press Incorporated
814 North Franklin Street
Chicago, Illinois 60610
ISBN 978-1-61373-487-2

Library of Congress Cataloging-in-Publication Data
Names: Browne, John Henry, 1946– author.
Title: The devil's defender: my odyssey through American criminal justice from Ted Bundy to the Kandahar massacre/John Henry Browne.
Description: Chicago, Illinois: Chicago Review Press Incorporated, 2016. | Includes index. | Description based on print version record and CIP data provided by publisher; resource not viewed.
Identifiers: LCCN 2015050333 (print) | LCCN 2015050255 (ebook) | ISBN 9781613734889 (pdf) | ISBN 9781613734896 (epub) | ISBN 9781613734902 (Kindle) | ISBN 9781613734872 (cloth: alk. paper)
Subjects: LCSH: Browne, John Henry, 1946– author. | Lawyers—United States—Biography.
Classification: LCC KF373.B76 (print) | LCC KF373.B76 A3 2016 (ebook) | DDC 340.092—dc23
LC record available at http://lccn.loc.gov/2015050333

Interior design: PerfecType, Nashville, TN
Interior layout: Nord Compo

Printed in the United States of America
5 4 3 2 1

**For Deborah Beeler and all victims of senseless crimes—
and all victims of an imperfect justice system.**

They thought that it would be a disgrace to go forth as a group. Each entered the forest at a point that he himself had chosen, where it was darkest and there was no path. If there is a path it is someone else's path and you are not on the adventure.

—Joseph Campbell, *The Hero's Journey*

CONTENTS

PROLOGUE

On an unusually clear morning in May 2012 I took the ferry from Bainbridge Island, where I had lived for the past twenty-three years, to Seattle, where I've had a private law practice since the 1970s. From the ferry terminal I drove to the studio of Q13, the local Fox TV affiliate. Over the years reporters from all over the world had interviewed me on camera, but this was going to be different. Host C. R. Douglas would be asking me questions I had declined to answer for three decades. The subject would be my most notorious client, the sociopath and mass murderer Theodore Robert Bundy.

The decision to break my silence did not come easily. My counsel of Bundy has always been a complicated matter in my career and personal life. When I was twenty-nine years old I sat with Ted in a jail cell in Florida and he confessed things to me he said he'd never told anyone else. Finally, as I was about to leave his cell, he stopped me. He had one more confession to add: the reason he'd consulted me as a lawyer for so long—nearly five years—was because we were "so much alike." I remember returning to my cheap motel room, lighting a cigarette, and looking at my reflection in the bathroom mirror. I felt sick to my stomach.

Bundy's assertion, which of course I've never agreed with or even understood, nonetheless grinded at me for years. So much so that I avoided even thinking about the conversation. My memory of it, I hoped, would never be tapped again.

Recently, though, as I've thought and wrote about other events in my life, Ted and his words kept bubbling up. I made the mistake of digging out from storage "the Ted box," which contained Bundy's case files as well as numerous letters he had sent me. Many of the old feelings of disgust and resentment came rushing back.

At the same time two new cases had thrown me back into the international spotlight. First, I took on, pro bono, the case of Colton Harris-Moore, the teenager known as the Barefoot Bandit, who'd been accused of breaking into countless homes, stealing airplanes, and leading authorities on a two-year manhunt that extended from western Washington State to the Caribbean.

Second, and also pro bono, I had accepted as a client Sgt. Robert Bales, accused of performing a solo raid on two Afghan villages on March 11, 2012. Bales allegedly shot, knifed, and in some cases burned innocent men, women, and children. Military prosecutors charged him with sixteen counts of first-degree murder, but the government's case seemed shaky to me from the start, largely because Bales was on his fourth deployment in almost as many years and was clearly suffering from posttraumatic stress disorder. He was also under the influence of steroids, which his superiors had provided. "If Sergeant Bales did it," I told anyone who would listen, "and I do mean *if*, we as a nation are to blame. We created this situation."

Despite the weight and obvious intrigue of these two cases, reporters would invariably bring up Ted Bundy, a topic I didn't want to discuss. But slowly I came to suspect that maybe, finally, it was time, that perhaps the public deserved to understand not only who Ted Bundy was but also why I and other criminal defense lawyers feel so duty bound to protect the rights of those accused of the most heinous crimes.

I decided to put pen to paper and open up about a life and career that included a leading role in the anti–Vietnam War movement, bringing awareness to the plight of battered women, and fighting for civil rights for prisoners, as well as my brushes with (as a fellow musician) the likes of the Grateful Dead and Jimi Hendrix and (as a member of the media) the Nixon administration. I would also talk about my work in some of the biggest criminal cases of the past forty years, including that of murder suspect David Kunze—when I put the forensic "science" of ear prints on trial—the Wah Mee massacre, and others, each seemingly more bizarre than the last.

I'd resolved to begin the process at this television studio on the shore of Seattle's Lake Union, answering C. R. Douglas's questions about Ted. I knew Douglas and I would only touch the surface. The biggest thing to come out would be that Bundy, whom history remembers as killing about thirty women, confessed to me that he had killed more than one hundred people, and not just women. I would describe a phone conversation I had with Ted shortly after his second escape from custody. And I would reveal that my former girlfriend had been murdered in a manner similar to a Ted Bundy victim.

That would be it. The rest is too big to fit into a twenty-five-minute conversation—partly because Ted told me so much more, but mostly because the story is larger and more complex than just Ted Bundy.

I have been thrown in jail myself. I have been a drug addict. I have been married more times than I care to tell you. But I have also followed a passion for justice and freedom since I was a child. I have won cases everyone else thought were impossible to win. I have defended innocent people. And I have defended monsters who nonetheless still deserved the fair trial our Constitution promises.

I stepped onto the set. A studio tech stuck a microphone in my left breast pocket. I sat across from C. R. Douglas, who looked out from a pair of horn-rimmed glasses, the glare of a klieg light bouncing off his impressive domelike head. The set behind us, seemingly lit with every conceivable shade of blue, convulsed in the manner known to anyone who watches cable news. Douglas looked at his notes. Then back at me. He asked the first question and waited for me to speak. I said what I could.

I'm going to tell you the rest here. While much of it, I hope, will be fun to read, we need to understand each other right now, from the top. A lot of this isn't going to be pretty.

I won't flinch if you won't.

1

THE TED MURDERS

That's all we had. A name. Women had vanished from Seattle and the surrounding region all year. And at first there was no way to talk about it—a woman, usually in her late teens or early twenties, would disappear and that was it: empty space where a promising young person had been. Aside from all the synonyms for fear, we had no language with which to discuss it. And then we did.

The *Seattle Times*, July 17, 1974, top of the fold: MISSING WOMAN LEFT BEACH WITH MAN, SAY WITNESSES. The article described the disappearance, three days earlier, of Denise Naslund, nineteen, and Janice Ott, twenty-three, at Lake Sammamish State Park. They were the eighth and ninth women to disappear in six months. Witnesses said the man had an injured arm and had asked the women for help loading a small sailboat onto his car. They described him, according to the newspaper, as "about 5 feet 6 or 7 inches, with a medium build and blondish-brown hair 'down to his neck.' He wore expensive-looking white tennis shoes, socks, shorts, and T-shirt. He also was described as smooth-talking with a 'small English accent.'"

But the next detail would prove the most critical. The witnesses said they overheard the man tell Janice Ott that his name was Ted.

Although the police were quoted as saying these disappearances were unrelated to the seven others, they would quickly change their minds, and the fear that had gripped Seattle soon had a title, a monosyllable you'd hear whispered in conversation all over the city—on the sidewalk, in the checkout line, the elevator. No one, it seemed, could avoid talking about it. Everywhere it was Ted, Ted, Ted.

As the new chief trial attorney with the King County Office of Public Defense, I had just moved to Seattle from Olympia, where I'd spent the two previous years working in the Washington State attorney general's office. But like everyone else, I'd followed the missing woman cases in the media since the beginning. The story seemed to have started not with a disappearance but with a University of Washington student savagely beaten.

Near campus on the morning of January 4, 1974, roommates found Karen Sparks, eighteen, unconscious in her bed. Blood covered the sheets. She'd been beaten with a metal rod and raped with some sort of shaft or dowel.

Just blocks away, on February 1, Lynda Ann Healy disappeared from her basement bedroom. On March 12 Donna Manson left her dorm to attend a concert at Evergreen State

College in Olympia and was never seen again. April 17 Susan Rancourt vanished from Central Washington State College in Ellensburg, a hundred miles east of Seattle. At Oregon State University in Corvallis, Roberta Parks disappeared on May 6, followed in quick succession by Brenda Ball (June 1) in Burien, just south of Seattle, and Georgeann Hawkins (June 11), apparently kidnapped as she walked down an alley directly behind her Kappa Theta Alpha sorority house at the University of Washington.

Now Denise Naslund and Janice Ott had vanished in front of thousands of witnesses. (July 14, 1974, was an uncommonly hot and cloud-free day in western Washington, and people had come out in droves to soak up the sun on the beaches of Lake Sammamish.) The nine women had much in common. They were all pretty and nearly all college students, and all wore their hair long, mostly parted down the middle, which in 1974 was the fashion. Women began to cut their hair short that summer, presumably to avoid abduction. Investigators fielded hundreds of tips from people who thought they might know "Ted." People turned in their friends, their coworkers, their boyfriends. If your name was Ted or Theodore in King County in the summer of 1974 and you drove a Volkswagen Bug—another detail witnesses were able to provide about the man at Lake Sammamish—the police likely knew about you. The lead detectives on the case called themselves the Ted Task Force. All their leads came up empty.

Then, just as abruptly as the abductions started, they stopped. There were no more disappearances after Naslund and Ott. The cease in activity was as eerie as it was relieving. But hysteria rose anew in early September when bird hunters found an open grave in the woods two miles southeast of Lake Sammamish. Investigators identified the skeletal remains of Naslund and Ott and uncovered dozens of other bones. They would later discover the remains of four victims—Ball, Healy, Parks, and Rancourt—on nearby Taylor Mountain, including skulls that showed blunt force trauma.

And that was it. After months of no abductions, police assumed that the killer had died, been incarcerated on another charge, or moved somewhere else.

Just as the Pacific Northwest shed its abduction problem, the state of Utah gained one. On October 2, 1974, sixteen-year-old Nancy Wilcox went missing from a neighborhood in a Salt Lake City suburb. Two and a half weeks later seventeen-year-old Melissa Anne Smith disappeared from another. On October 18 another seventeen-year-old, Laura Aime, was apparently snatched in Lehi, thirty miles south of Salt Lake.

On November 8 Carol DaRonch, a pretty nineteen-year-old telephone operator with brown hair parted down the middle, steered her maroon Camaro into the parking lot of Fashion Place Mall, the biggest shopping center in Salt Lake Valley. It was Friday night, and the place was packed. She found a parking spot in front of Sears, locked her car, and entered the mall. At a window display at Walden Books, a tall man with a mustache and a head of thick hair approached her. He introduced himself as Officer Rosebud and said he believed her car had been broken into. She needed to come with him to identify a suspect his partner had detained in the parking lot. She thought she smelled alcohol on his breath, but she explained it away in her mind when he flashed her what looked like a police badge.

Carol followed Rosebud out to her Camaro, which looked as if it hadn't been touched since she left it half an hour earlier. There was no partner and no suspect. Officer Rosebud insisted she accompany him across the street to the "police substation," the door of which was inexplicably behind a Laundromat. When the door wouldn't open—it was locked—he insisted that she accompany him to the Murray police station. She followed him to what had to be the most decrepit police car ever issued to an officer: a banged-up VW Bug with torn upholstery.

Against better judgment, Carol climbed into the passenger seat, and Officer Rosebud drove them eastbound, which Carol knew didn't lead to the police station. Suddenly he flipped a U-turn, stopped the car, and brandished a pair of handcuffs. He quickly cuffed her left wrist, and when she struggled to break free he inadvertently snapped the second cuff on the same wrist. She fumbled for the door handle, and he raised what looked like a metal pipe and swung it at her head. She dodged the blow and ran out into oncoming traffic. A car stopped, and the passenger door opened. Carol dove across the lap of its passengers, a married couple.

By then the VW was long gone.

An hour later, about twenty miles north of the mall, Debra Kent, seventeen, disappeared after a play at Viewmont High School. Witnesses reported seeing a handsome, if suspicious, man with a moustache lurking around the school before the play.

The abductions spread east into Colorado, where between January 12, 1975, and April 6, 1975, three women, all in their twenties, went missing, including twenty-three-year-old Caryn Campbell, who disappeared from a ski resort near Aspen. May and June saw the youngest victims to date, a twelve-year-old in Pocatello, Idaho, and a fifteen-year-old in Provo, Utah.

Slowly, the authorities in the western states began to connect the dots. The kidnappings, and the few bodies that had been recovered, seemed too similar not to be related. Could the "Ted" that terrorized the Seattle region in the first half of 1974 be the same man stalking the young women and teenagers of Colorado and Utah?

Decades later retired Utah highway patrolman Robert Hayward would tell a *Deseret News* reporter he thought it was an act of "the Lord"—the wrong turn he took at 3:00 AM on August 16, 1975, in his own neighborhood, placing the Volkswagen in the beam of his headlights. The Bug sat in front of the suburban home of two teenagers Hayward knew and whose parents he knew were out of town.

The suspicious car bolted away, and Hayward pursued it for several blocks before it pulled over at an abandoned gas station. A man popped out of the car and said, "I'm lost." He wore a black turtleneck, and his dark hair curled down the length of his neck. He said he was a second-year law student at the University of Utah and, at Hayward's request, handed over his driver's license: Theodore Robert Bundy, age twenty-eight.

When the man couldn't explain what he was doing in the neighborhood at that hour to Hayward's satisfaction, the patrolman got his permission—later contested—to look inside the car. The search revealed two pairs of handcuffs, an ice pick, a crowbar, panty hose, and a ski mask. A sheriff's deputy arrived and arrested Bundy on suspicion of burglary.

Detectives soon connected Bundy to the DaRonch kidnapping nearly a year earlier, as well as the multiple missing persons investigations. Then, over the next few weeks, more dots as they consulted the Ted Task Force in Seattle. All agreed: they had found "Ted." Bolstered by the positive lineup identification of abduction survivor Carol DaRonch—also later contested—Utah authorities charged Bundy with kidnapping.

Soon out on bail—it had been set for $100,000, unusually low given the nature of the crime—and bound for Seattle, where he was now the Ted Task Force's top suspect, Bundy called two friends whom he'd met while working on Washington governor Dan Evans's recent election. They were attorney Marlin Vortman and another attorney, who is now a judge and wishes to remain anonymous (we'll refer to him as "Nick" here).

Bundy told Nick and Marlin there'd been a mix-up, a stupid little problem in Utah, he said, a total misunderstanding, and asked if they knew of a good criminal defense attorney. They said they knew just the man, a new up-and-coming defense attorney in Seattle who, like them, recently worked with the governor's office.

Then Marlin and Nick offered a warning, one important consideration. Five years earlier in California, they said, the defense lawyer's twenty-three-year-old girlfriend was murdered. *He might be sensitive about defending someone implicated in the homicide of young women.*

Bundy thought about that for just a beat. "That's the guy I want."

2

"WHERE'D YOU GET THOSE SHOES?"

Marlin called me in October 1975. I knew him and Nick through my former job at the attorney general's office, and I respected them both, as well as their boss, Governor Dan Evans. Marlin asked if I was aware of the Bundy investigation and if I would be willing to help. I said "Sure" but reminded him I was only three years out of law school. He said Ted had "researched" me and desired my help.

Coincidentally, on the same day, and unrelated to my conversation with Marlin, the King County Office of Public Defense officially assigned me Bundy's case. It was their policy at the time to assign an attorney to a case even if it was in the investigation stage and there were no charges.

Ted, Marlin, Nick, and I convened later that day in my office. News crews had followed Ted to my building, and Marlin and Nick had to slip in through a side door. Ted entered waving and joking with reporters. When he told my receptionist who he was, the lobby cleared out and my receptionist, Brenda, quit on the spot.

I was immediately struck by Ted's appearance. He wore a turtleneck sweater under a corduroy jacket, khakis, and Bass Weejun loafers. The look seemed to be an attempt to telegraph "Ivy League law student." But it was a caricature of an Ivy League law student.

He referred to the charges in Salt Lake as "this little stupid" case in Utah. I told him there was a much bigger problem. The Seattle newspapers were running headlines such as IS THE UTAH TED THE SEATTLE TED? He scoffed, saying, "If they haven't put it together by now, they never will." I found this chilling and, frankly, way too much information.

The day after my highly publicized meeting with Bundy, detective Robert Keppel, who'd established and co-led the Ted Task Force, called me to say, "In a case of this magnitude the attorney-client privilege should not apply." He wanted me to provide him with evidence against my client! I laughed and suggested he reread the Bill of Rights.

Another of the Seattle detectives working the case was Roger Dunn, whom I'd known from previous cases. He was friendly and smart, the kind of person Ted would like. Despite my telling the police Ted would not talk, Roger stopped over at Ted's house "just to chat." Ted invited him in and promptly called me. I was polite but told Roger to leave, which he did.

He did have time for coffee though, and Ted, as usual, asked the questions and answered none.

Frustrated with the investigation, Detective Keppel put a tail on Ted, who took to wearing fake beards and moustaches to fool the cops. He would taunt them by making them sandwiches and offering them coffee and advice on how to lie low during stakeouts.

At one point I arranged for Ted to take a lie detector test, which he failed. He said he was sure he would pass because his "personality type" could fool the machine. I asked why he needed to fool the machine if he was innocent, and he said it was just a game.

He used my office law library to research arrest and search and seizure laws. He became an expert on the fallibility of eyewitness identification. Experts know well that eyewitness testimony is the weakest form of evidence but is powerful in front of a jury or judge. You know, that "I will never forget that face" kind of stuff. Of course there was not just the identification by DaRonch in Utah; there was also the very odd and sinister stuff found in his car. And his passenger seat was loose and facing backward. This is the kind of circumstantial evidence that is much more powerful than eyewitness testimony. Therefore Ted filed numerous motions to dismiss the case for his "illegal" arrest—denied—and to suppress the evidence found in his car—also denied.

During these visits to my office, I could see Ted trying to get closer and closer to me. He knew I was only four months older than he was, and the similarity in our ages seemed like a big deal to him. He started asking where I purchased my clothing and what books, movies, and television shows I enjoyed. If I told him I'd bought, say, my penny loafers at The Bon Marché, the next time I saw him, swear to god, he'd be wearing the same penny loafers. I embarrassed him once when he arrived with *actual* pennies tucked into the shoe creases. I laughed and said, "Ted, that hasn't been a thing since the early 1960s."

He would also call my house at night, which caused me to lose more than one girlfriend. They'd answer my home phone, hear, "This is Ted Bundy. Is John there?" and leave.

There was so much hysteria surrounding Ted. Women again began getting their hair cut short and dyed so as not to look like one of his potential victims. People saw him behind every tree and bush. On December 5, 1975, I received the following letter from the dean of the University of Washington law school:

> Dear Mr. Browne and Mr. Bundy:
> This is in response to your communication of December 3, 1975, requesting permission to use the Law Library to pursue legal research in which you are engaged.
>
> By regulation, the Law Library of the University is open to any person having need to use legal maintained in the Library. Hence, I have no basis to purport to either grant or deny you permission to use the Library.
>
> We have a substantial number of women students and staff regularly in the Library. You may care to consider whether the apprehensions which some of them may entertain as a result of the newspaper stories concerning you, even if unreasonable, might make it more comfortable from their

standpoint and yours if you used the County Law Library for your purposes.
Very truly yours,
Richard S. L. Roddis
Dean

Ted, his parents, and his friends came up with the funds to hire John O'Connell for his Utah defense. O'Connell was brash, aggressive, eccentric, and very, very good—the best criminal defense lawyer in the Beehive State. He put fear into the local police and prosecutors. He made pretrial motions to suppress evidence and motions to exclude alleged statements Ted made to authorities. He motioned to suppress Carol DaRonch's lineup ID. All the other men in the lineup were obviously cops, and DaRonch had seen Ted's photo before the lineup. Of course he looked familiar.

Ted seemed to be drawn to system fighters, and O'Connell, like me, was a system fighter. The three of us met in person and on the phone many times before Ted's Utah trial. Ted drew the judge everybody felt was the fairest, most courageous, and most honest in Utah. His name was Stewart Hanson, and he was his own man, not a good ole boy. It was John's idea to waive a jury trial and have a bench trial. This is always risky, as the defendant's fate is in the hands of one person, the judge, not twelve. All you need for a hung jury is one juror's vote. But the press had been sensational in both Washington and Utah, which meant it would be difficult, if not impossible, to get a fair jury. So John decided to go with Judge Hanson. The trial began on February 23, 1976.

The most important decision in any trial, with the possible exception of whether to have a judge or jury trial, is whether the defendant should testify. Thanks to the Fifth Amendment, defendants have the right to not incriminate themselves. Some defendants, particularly those who are sympathetic enough to gain the jury's and judge's confidence and goodwill, can help themselves by testifying; but get a defendant who's clearly lying or whose icy demeanor will turn off the courtroom, and you've got a problem. Ted decided to go on the stand, and he did so contrary to O'Connell's advice. "This fucking idiot wants to go on the stand," O'Connell said. Then, exasperated, "Oh fuck you, Ted. Do what you want." Ted believed he could lie his way out of anything and could charm the judge. He was wrong. He was caught in lies that he had never been to Colorado, that he didn't possess numerous license plates. He also had to explain why he had such a bizarre collection of items in his car. He should never have testified. There was too much to explain away.

His family and friends were in attendance on March 1 when Judge Hanson pronounced Ted guilty of attempted kidnapping and remanded him to custody. On June 30 Ted gave an emotional plea for leniency. Judge Hanson was unconvinced, but he did levy a relatively light sentence since Ted was a first-time offender. Under this sentence he could be free within eighteen months.

I wrote to Ted and warned him not to get attached to his release date, as the investigations in Washington and Colorado were heating up. I had no idea at the time that this was only the beginning of my work with him. He responded in characteristic fashion: there was nothing to worry about because there were no strong cases against him.

It amazed me that any sane person would believe he could overcome the mountain of evidence the state had presented. Ted was perceptive when it came to everything but his self-image.

It was that same blind spot that caused him to misapprehend our relationship. He thought we were friends. He thought that because we dressed alike and had similar interests—women, cars, the law—we were cut from the same cloth.

But really Ted Bundy knew nothing about me. He didn't know who my family was. He didn't know where I was from. And he sure as shit didn't know anything about the events that led me to where I was.

3

THE SHADOWS OF SECRET CITIES

Harry Browne was always in motion. Hell, as a member of the New York State Corps of Engineers, the man studied motion. So he surprised no one that bright morning in June 1943 when he bolted from the Syracuse hospital where his wife had just given birth to their first child. He was headed home for a quick shower. He'd done the calculations. Said he'd be back before his wife woke up.

A decade earlier, at Staten Island's Curtis High School, he'd fallen hard for Helen Brightsen, daughter of Arnt Brightsen, a Norwegian merchant marine captain who jumped ship only to captain janitors for a local school district. Harry was smart. Helen was smarter. A National Merit Scholar, she read multiple newspapers every day and could understand any math equation, no matter how complex. Her father was unimpressed; he said a woman didn't belong where men were. Said he'd only pay for college if she applied herself to be a nurse or teacher. Harry, whose father was a Staten Island dock worker, was different. Harry loved Helen's mind. They dated all through high school and married in 1937. He enrolled at Manhattan College and studied engineering—his heart set on building roads and bridges—and soon landed a job with New York State. Now he and Helen had a family: a daughter, Bonnie, just hours old.

At home Harry stepped out of the shower in time to hear the phone ring. Figured it was either a family friend calling to congratulate him or family back at the hospital announcing that Helen was awake.

The man on the other end of the line introduced himself as Col. James C. Marshall, the military lead on a new government-funded engineering program. What exactly the program was, the colonel couldn't say. It was secret. But it was a once-in-a-lifetime opportunity for a twenty-two-year-old man with a new family. Would Harry be interested? *Yes? Good. See you in Tennessee in three days.*

And so Harry, Helen, and baby Bonnie were on the move—from New York down through Pennsylvania, across Virginia, through Knoxville, and into Oak Ridge, population three thousand and growing by the hundreds every day.

Guard towers surrounded the town, as did several miles of chain-link and barbwire fence. Harry and Helen rolled up to one of seven entry gates, where soldiers searched their car before waving them in. Children played in the streets. Folks lined up outside a movie theater, just like in Anywhere, USA, in the 1940s. But when Harry and Helen looked closer they noticed that nearly every adult wore a name badge. The houses (white, Spartan, brand new) were nearly identical. They spotted a billboard on which a cartoonish Uncle Sam rolled up his sleeves; below him were three monkeys, one covering its eyes, another its ears, and a third its lips. Underneath were the words WHAT YOU SEE HERE, WHAT YOU DO HERE, WHAT YOU HEAR HERE, WHEN YOU LEAVE HERE, LET IT STAY HERE. Another billboard read THE ENEMY IS LOOKING FOR INFORMATION. GUARD YOUR TALK.

The Brownes settled into one of the small houses, and Harry reported to Colonel Marshall. Oak Ridge, Harry had learned, was conceived shortly after the Japanese bombed Pearl Harbor on December 7, 1941, and the United States declared war on Japan and Germany. Harry and a team of physicists and chemists would be developing methods for enriching uranium to create a weapon like no other.

I was born three years later, on August 11, 1946. By then the work at Oak Ridge—the combined efforts of some twenty-two thousand employees—had come to fruition. With the enriched uranium from Oak Ridge and other locations, J. Robert Oppenheimer developed an atomic bomb, and the United States dropped two such weapons on Japan, in Hiroshima and Nagasaki, in 1945, killing as many as 246,000 people, effectively ending the war.

I have no memory of Oak Ridge, but there is a photo of me from that time. I've just turned one, and I'm sitting outside in a high chair eating birthday cake with my hands. Behind me the identical barracks of the compound line the street. We were gone within months.

Harry was on the move again. The Atomic Energy Commission had big plans for my dad. So we yo-yoed around the country: Oak Ridge, Tennessee, to Washington, DC, to Palo Alto, California, to Albuquerque, New Mexico, to Cleveland, Ohio, to La Jolla, California, and back to Palo Alto.

It was in Albuquerque where some of my earliest (and fondest) memories formed. We lived at the very edge of the city, near the foothills of the Sandia Mountains. What a gift to be young and in the middle of Wonderland. I had reptile friends—toads, lizards, and snakes. I'd hold them and wonder at their ability to live and thrive in the desert, then let them go. Trapdoor spiders intrigued me for hours as I would discover their well-hidden homes and wait for them to emerge and close the door. I remember feeling I was a small part of the universe, sharing the privilege of life with these creatures.

The foothills were full of natural caves, some burrowed into the Sandias themselves. I discovered Native American pottery remnants (I still have one), smoke-stained walls, and lots of old stuff. A faded magazine, something like *Soldier of Fortune*, extolled the virtues of justice, Saudi Arabia style: a photo of a beheading and an alleged thief's hand cut off. It made me sick to my stomach and cry. I had heard what the Nazis did and seen some TV about the Holocaust, but their brutality was not as clear to me as these images in the magazine. How could I be in rapture in New Mexico while across the world people were cutting off heads and hands?

I also found shell casings, old newspapers, a quill pen, the top of a silver train conductor's watch, and pictures of nude women. I was ten or eleven years old and very unworldly. The porn was lightweight by today's standards but piqued my interest. I brought one of the photos home to show my sister, three years my senior, to ask for an explanation. She tore it up and told me to ask our dad about it.

I loved my dad, but he was hard to talk to and had all kinds of rigid rules. If I used a screwdriver and didn't put it back in the exact specified spot and he noticed, I was no longer allowed to use any tool, ever. Once on a road trip in the family's '54 Bel Air I got motion sickness and puked so hard it splashed onto the turquoise felt ceiling. (Because we lived in the Southwest, he insisted the automobile he drove be white and turquoise.) He stopped the car to inspect the damage: a big splatter he tried to clean but that left a stain for years. He stayed angry just as long.

So no, I wasn't going to ask him about a naked woman's photo I'd found in a weird desert cave. He never did speak to me about sex and instead left me to learn about it at school and through the gossip of my male classmates.

New Mexico is also where I began my lifelong love affair with shadows. The long, distinct shadows of late afternoon are my favorite, full of power and beauty. Seeing yourself in a shadow is nothing like seeing yourself in a mirror. The smallest twig sticking up from the sand in a New Mexico late afternoon casts a long shadow and, to me, reveals the true power of the twig. The same was true when I viewed my own dark image elongated in the warm sand.

Later I read about Hiroshima and the bomb we dropped—the bomb that my own father had a hand in developing. I learned that the nuclear explosion left shadows cast by its light, that the silhouettes of nuked Japanese people were discovered on walls days after the detonation.

When I asked my dad about Hiroshima he gave me a look, a *We don't talk about that* look. But I've never been able to get those shadows out of my mind, not the benevolent shadows of my New Mexico desert or the shadows of the Japanese whom we, as a country, killed in a flash of light.

By the time I turned twelve we had moved to La Jolla, California. To my surprise, I was popular with the other kids. This corresponded with my budding interest in politics, ignited when I met Senator John Kennedy, then a candidate for president. My father was a delegate to the Democratic Convention in Los Angeles, and I got to shake the senator's hand. He also gave me a signed business card. Our family became instant Kennedy junkies. We loved him and his Camelot. My sister wore her hair like Jackie's, and I affected a Boston accent. We thought the world would be safe and kind, just as long as the Kennedys were in charge.

So I decided to run for student body president of La Jolla Junior High School. I ran thinking that if I won, my parents would not move me to Palo Alto—where my dad had a new position—until tenth grade. I was right—this manipulative ploy worked, but it caused stress in the family with my dad living in Palo Alto and the rest of us in La Jolla for nine months.

When we all did eventually move, in June 1961, it was front-page news in *Hi-Tide*, the student paper: "John Browne, president of the freshman class, will move to Palo Alto, Calif. after school closes. . . . He regrets having to leave, he said. . . . He is also a member of Boys' Federation Council, in which he handles the 'Boy of the Week' program, and he is a member of the Youth Hostel. Golf and tennis are John's favorite sports."

Because its student body consisted of the sons and daughters of Stanford professors, Palo Alto High School was extraordinary—so many smart kids. But I was not one of them. I was average in scholastics, but I was an observer, absorbing all the town had to offer.

I soon learned there were two Palo Altos: the relatively mainstream Palo Alto of Stanford and a more underground, shadowy part of the city. There were readings in the local bookstores by Lawrence Ferlinghetti and Allen Ginsberg, so I went to see what a beatnik looked like, and smoked a tobacco pipe (and looked stupid doing so) and got sick. Ferlinghetti's City Lights bookstore in San Francisco was just a short train ride away, as were the other sins of North Beach: topless dancers and female impersonators. At the time I assumed this was going on all across America. (Until I left California, I didn't even know there was such a thing as a Young Republican.)

I got a job washing dishes at Saint Michael's Alley on University Avenue, next door to the Varsity Theater. The owners told me that one night Ginsberg had stood on a table and began, in a drug-induced trance of some kind, to recite his poem "Howl" until he fell to the floor. Ken Kesey lived on nearby Skyline Boulevard and gave the Hells Angels acid before they drove down University Avenue right in front of the café, blasted out of their minds.

And there was a Stanford professor, whose daughter I hung out with, experimenting with LSD and creating quite a fuss on the Stanford campus. He and his wife were also pioneers of the sexual revolution and kept copies of *Eros* magazine on the coffee table. I loved that magazine. I still do.

At school I got along with all the cliques—preppies, jocks, greasers, it didn't matter. One day a greaser by the name of Ron McKernan came into one of my classes and, in a fit of rage, picked up a desk to throw at the teacher. Not a chair, a *desk*. He was looking for a friend, and when the teacher demanded he leave, Ron got mad. I intervened, calmed him down, and talked him into setting the desk back on the floor. After that we became, if not friends, friendly. He went by the nickname Pigpen and was a vocalist and keyboard player in the most innovative band in town, the Warlocks, which would eventually become the Grateful Dead. In fact multiple musicians associated with the Dead went to Palo Alto High.

I got along with all the cliques, but I belonged to none. At least one thing made it impossible for me to fit in: I had a job. Make that two jobs. In addition to washing dishes at Saint Michael's a few nights a week, on Saturdays I worked at Spiro's Sport Shop in the shopping center next to the high school. I was the only kid I knew from this upscale high school who worked. I was not from a poor family, we were always middle class, but I wanted the freedom of earning my own money. No control or hooks from the parents.

I once asked my dad if he'd buy me a car, and he said not until I got all As and Bs on my report card. I was close but not there yet. When he and my mother went to Europe for a month, I seized the opportunity to buy two vehicles: a 1952 Chevy panel truck completely rusted through and held together with bailing wire ($65) and a classic 1954 Austin-Healey Le Mans, a beautiful British sports car ($850). The Healy had a leather strap over the hood, and the windshield folded down for racing. It needed work, but I fixed it up and had it painted

British racing green. When I picked up my folks at the airport, took them home, and opened the garage, my dad saw the Healey and said, "I told you, no car until you had all As and Bs." I reminded him he said *he* would not buy me one but said nothing about buying my own.

This was the first of many times he'd accuse me of becoming a "damn lawyer."

The Palo Alto Playhouse was a very active center for the performing arts. I had one of the leads in *Rebel Without a Cause* (playing the bad guy), and I was Ice in *West Side Story*. Both of these productions involved handguns as props, which I provided, along with blanks, from Spiro's Sport Shop. I carried the pistols in my glove compartment, and my friends would pull them out and pretend to shoot each other walking down the main street, which obviously would never be acceptable today.

Speaking of guns, on Tuesdays and Thursdays I'd ride my ten-speed to school with my .22-caliber target rifle over my shoulder. I was on the rifle team and needed a weapon for after-school practice. I stored it in science class during the day. Now there would be a SWAT team descending on the school, or I'd have been shot on the way to campus.

I dated a girl named Bonnie—same as my sister—very briefly. Her father was blind. He worked at Stanford and had a watch whose face flipped open so he could feel its hands. I never got tired of watching him do that—this middle-aged guy sensing the passage of time at his fingertips.

He had a huge garage, which he generously allowed his daughter's friends to use for band practice. The first time I went to see the band practice I met Michael Kilmartin, the guitar player. He was tall like me, maybe six foot two, and funny as hell. We hit it off right away.

He didn't fit into any of the cliques either, although he was a superb athlete. He was on the track team—shot put and discus. His family had a gorgeous house on the Stanford campus, which was strange because they weren't rich. His dad was in the military. I don't know how they ended up with that house. It was an incredible Tudor house *on* campus. And Michael was brilliant. The whole family was. His ten-year-old brother, Alan, could draw like M. C. Escher and play "East-West," a complex piece that changes from Eastern to Western tempos and rhythms, on the guitar.

I only had one other close friend. Her name was Anne Babson, but everyone called her Punky. Our relationship was completely platonic. That makes it sound like I wasn't attracted to her, but that's not it. I actually really was, a lot. But it was very clear in the beginning that we were just going to be best friends. She was smart, had an artistic bent, and as a teenager was already taking stunning photographs.

Not fitting into any one group—but getting along with them all—had its advantages. It meant I didn't alienate any of them, and so just like in La Jolla, I had luck with student politics: I was elected class president.

That didn't bode well with administrators, who thought I would lead a faction of rebellious students. They had reason to worry. When Principal Ray Ruppel banned the popular FOOTHILL 69 T-shirts (from Foothill Community College) due to their "inappropriate" sexual reference, I used my skills as a silk screener to manufacture FOOTHILL 69½ T-shirts. Ruppel tried to discipline me for the stunt, but I pointed out to him that he only banned "69 shirts." (Interestingly, at the time I didn't even know what 69 meant.) But nothing prepared him for my next act of defiance.

On November 22, 1963, I stood behind a podium and presided over a student assembly in the auditorium. I was a senior, just six months away from graduation. Every student at Palo Alto High was looking at me, hanging on my every word. I had never felt more hopeful and in control of my future. Principal Ruppel materialized offstage and waved me over. I excused myself from the stage and walked up to him to ask what possible reason he could have for interrupting me.

He said President Kennedy had been assassinated. I froze. He told me it was my duty to inform the students. I refused. I didn't return to the stage. I walked out of the building and off campus and didn't return for days.

I headed for the mountains with classmates Rich Godfrey and Jeffie Page. The three of us broke into a shack in a closed ski area. It was easy to imagine the hut as part of a tiny city or village—but a village that had been abandoned, as if its inhabitants had left in a hurry, their hut-dwelling civilization having crumbled under the pressure of some unknown force. Rich and Jeffie thought we should drink the hope right out of us and passed a bottle around. JFK, the one leader we truly believed in, was gone.

Winter was approaching, and in the cold shack we sipped whiskey. I didn't drink much. (I actually hated alcohol, even though I knew it was uncool to; I used to pour beer all over me and try to act drunk.) The sky outside the window was a dull, overcast white. All the shadows had disappeared. There in the forest, exactly twenty years after my father had joined our country's effort to end World War II, and after our bombs killed all those people—and less than a decade after I fell in love with the desert and its shadows—the world looked ugly, drained of purpose.

I didn't know more war was coming. I didn't know war would always be coming. And I didn't know that my life would always be intimately tied to it and to death. For now I tipped back the bottle and observed Rich and Jeffie. They looked drunk. I wondered if I did.

4

"ARE YOU EXPERIENCED?"

It was only September, but the snow fell hard in the Mile High City when I got off the train and slogged my trunk to the University of Denver. I knocked on the door at Skyline Hall, an old apartment complex on campus. I was almost scared to see inside. The arrangement was four guys—me and three strangers—crammed into a two-bedroom space.

It was my dad who suggested I attend the University of Denver. He had spoken to some of his academic friends at Stanford and asked if they knew of a school for an average kid, not too smart but good-hearted. They told him DU was a good college with small classes and up-and-coming professors.

So on September 1, 1964, I left Palo Alto on the train. I didn't know anyone in Denver and had never been there. I just knew it was far away from home. The only thing I remember about the train ride was getting into an argument with some guy about Barry Goldwater. (I loved Goldwater's independence but despised his politics.)

At Skyline Hall a black guy answered the door. Back home, despite the town's liberal academic facade, African Americans lived on one small street or across the highway in East Palo Alto. There were only two or three black kids at Palo Alto High, and I didn't know them.

The guy at the door introduced himself as Steve Rhodes from Washington, DC. We shared a bedroom and quickly became friends. He and I later started the Denver chapter of Students for a Democratic Society (SDS) and were members of the Student Nonviolent Coordinating Committee (SNCC) and the Congress for Racial Equality (CORE). I was the only white person in the local chapter of CORE. (My dad didn't like my affiliation with these groups. Back in the 1950s he had seen people lose their government and civilian jobs after joining radical, left-wing groups. "You are throwing away your future," he told me more than once.)

But my dad's professor friends were right about DU. The school was a perfect fit for me. I had always done better in a small pool rather than the ocean. I grew to love studying. I learned to love books: the smell, the feel, the contents. DU has a beautiful old library—Tudor style with huge cracked leather chairs and green table lamps on rectangular oak reading tables. I spent hours in the main room and in the stacks. I actually had a brain, it turned out, and I could use it. To put it simply, I fell in love with learning.

But all through freshmen year I still had the nagging sense that I didn't fit in. That feeling reached a peak at a party at some rich guy's house, a sea of Brooks Brothers shirts and Bass penny loafers. They were listening to some music, the Mamas and the Papas, and I had this deep experience of not belonging. These were not the people I felt comfortable around or related to. Sure, I liked pink button-down shirts, still do, but the rest of the trust-fund scene was vapid and dull. I left the party and climbed a nearby tree. Up in the branches I realized I was homesick. I missed Michael. He was still in the Bay Area attending Foothill Community College on a track scholarship.

A few days later I checked with the athletic department at DU and asked if they'd be interested in Michael next year. I called Michael, and I put the two together. By the following fall he was at DU with me, on a track scholarship.

We rented an apartment. Man, it was fun. Michael loved Denver. He loved being away from home. We rented 50cc motor scooters at a gas station and took them up in the mountains, zipping around on the trails. Michael was the funniest person I've ever known in my life—lots of stuff that seems juvenile now but at the time had me laughing uncontrollably. We had a buffet line in the cafeteria at school, one of those all-you-can-eat types. There'd be a woman in front of him, a middle-aged woman, and he'd say, "Tickle your ass with a feather?"

And she'd turn around and go, "*What?*"

And he'd say, "Particularly nasty weather!"

One of the first things Michael wanted to do when he joined me in Colorado was start a band. He came home one afternoon with a fake Fender bass, ugly and poorly made. He shoved it into my lap and said he was going to teach me to play the bass for a new act he was forming, the Crystal Palace Guard. Two weeks later I was playing bass onstage. Our six-person band had a unique sound—blues, rock, folk—with a killer harmonica player, an amazing guitar player (Michael), and a female singer (Chris Williamson) who also played harpsichord.

We started out performing shows at bars in Aspen and Vail. No easy feat in the winter: a six-hour drive to Aspen over snowy Loveland Pass, ten thousand feet high, all six of us and our cheap equipment packed into a broken-down Corvair van (my new wheels) and Michael's Rambler station wagon.

We eventually signed on with two Denver promoters, Kent and Earl, who bought us expensive new equipment—Kustom amplifiers, a brand new House of Theatre PA system—and gave me money to purchase a real bass, a Gibson EB-0. They bought Chris Williamson a Baldwin electric harpsichord.

Within six months we were playing four to five nights a week all over Colorado, Wyoming, Kansas, New Mexico, and once in Texas. At the same time we were all in college full time and pulling A and B averages. The pay was very little at first, $100 split six ways, but as we gained more attention and acceptance we sometimes made $750 to $1,500 per week.

Kent and Earl were also the main concert producers in and around Denver. They teamed up with Chet Helm, who owned The Family Dog—an influential venue in San Francisco—and set up shop in an old ballroom in Denver that he called—what else?—The Family Dog. Helms and his partners put a lot of money into the building, and it was beautiful, with a top-notch sound system and a professional platform for the obligatory light show. He even imported talent from San Francisco to run the lights.

All the big acts played there: the Doors, Big Brother and the Holding Company, the Grateful Dead, Them with Van Morrison, and the Kinks. Our band opened for a lot of those groups, and we sometimes played with them in the park during the daytime. A *Denver Post* piece about a July 30, 1967, show in Washington Park reviewed us more favorably than the Dead and Captain Beefheart. Of course this wasn't accurate. No way were we better than those guys. But the local band got the local love. The press referred to the Crystal Palace Guard as Denver's answer to Jefferson Airplane.

Unlike the rest of the band, I wasn't a real musician, but my organizational skills and technical know-how secured my spot. I could fix almost any problem with the amplifiers and sound system, and I made sure we got to the jobs on time and not too stoned. After a few problems I instituted an "If you're wired, you're fired" policy, only breaking it a few times myself. (Once while performing at Colorado State University, I was so blessed by the ganja, I stopped playing to listen to how beautiful the music was. Michael yelled at me after a few minutes, and I started playing again.)

The Doors played at The Family Dog on September 29, 1967. I sat on the floor with Jim Morrison in the greenroom as he wrote poetry on toilet paper and paper towels. He was, as usual, withdrawn, sullen, and drunk—no drugs, just a lot of alcohol. Kent and Earl had tasked me with babysitting the Lizard King.

He refused to play until he got more alcohol. The stores were closed, so I went around to all my college friends' homes and returned with an assortment of cheap college-kid booze: Spanada and other fortified wine. He drank it all, much of it from both sides of his mouth at once, and stumbled onstage with his trademark white cotton peasant shirt and tight black leather pants. We surrounded the stage and had orders to jump him if he started taking his clothes off. The police were also next to the stage awaiting orders from one Detective Love, a Denver Police Department narc who sniffed around the periphery of all our activities. (The light show would flash WELCOME BROTHER LOVE to warn of his presence whenever he showed up.)

Morrison did a few numbers and then lurched into "Break on Through," sticking his hands down his pants to rub his very noticeable hard-on as he looked at a beautiful young woman in the crowd and said, "Be my hand!" He fell on the stage and began to scream the lyrics as he was mounting the floor, the microphone, and the stage lights. He made it through the night without getting arrested, and it was a breathtaking performance.

On Valentine's Day 1968 Kent and Earl put on a Jimi Hendrix show at Regis College in Denver, and I was given the thankless job of running the PA system without enough or adequate equipment. Hendrix got mad at me but finished the show. As usual I was also given the job of babysitting.

Michael, Michael's girlfriend Mary, and I took Jimi and one of his roadies all over Denver so they could find drugs. In Larimer Square they found what they wanted: heroin. Jimi was, like Morrison, obsessed with sex and women. We had to protect Mary and many other women during our two-day babysitting job.

While in Larimer Square, Mary, Michael, Jimi, and I came across a Native American antique store. (The roadie headed to a bar.) Michael and I waited outside while Mary and Jimi went into the store. Jimi returned with the most beautiful antique Navajo Concho belt, which had cost him $5,000. I took a photo of Michael, Mary, and Jimi with the belt. (He appeared with the belt in concert photos and on album covers after that.) More than a decade later my connection to Hendrix and that day would come up again in an extraordinary moment in Seattle. But that's a story for later.

I was about to have some troubles. The first came courtesy of the US military. I was a student and had a student deferment, which should have kept me out of the draft. And I don't know if it was because of my involvement with a hippie band or with SDS, SNCC, and CORE, but I lost my deferment. So, incidentally, did my friend and former roommate Steve Rhodes, with whom I'd founded the local chapter of SDS. We got reclassified the same week.

Home on a holiday break, I reported to the military induction center in Oakland. I had decided before the draft notice that I would not serve in Vietnam and would go to Canada, Mexico, or jail if I had to. Lefty *Ramparts* magazine and the *New Republic* were my bibles, and the "teach-ins" I had attended educated me about the war and how wrong it was. The body counts, on both sides, were in the hundreds every week. I could not kill anybody and was not so hot about the idea of getting killed. Two of my high school classmates had already died, both minorities who had volunteered. I became an expert on induction rules and regulations, with the aid of many antiwar organizations, mostly the Quaker Church.

Maybe my political activism had something to do with my reclassification. Maybe it didn't. I'll never know. But when I arrived at my physical, I was put on the infamous Group W bench, immortalized in the Arlo Guthrie song "Alice's Restaurant." It was a special bench reserved for those with serious physical or mental health problems, religious objectors, and gay men.

I came armed with letters from two doctors attesting that I was unfit to kill small people, as I was six foot seven. The draft criteria excluded anyone taller than six foot six. I presented my letters to some beefy officer who called out my name for special attention. Hair down to my shoulders, a thick 'stache spread across my face, I looked like central casting for "antiwar hippie," and I was smug because I knew the law. The officer read the letters and said, "Come with me. We'll get you measured." I imagined some sort of reverse rack that would shrink me to under six six. They made me take off my shoes and socks and tried to press my feet to the floor, pushing my arches down.

I was still well over six six. The pit bull–looking induction officer led me to an office. He informed me that I could apply for a waiver to circumvent the height restriction. I said, "You mean you want me to get a waiver so I can go to Vietnam and kill little people? In a war I don't believe in? No thank you."

I was reclassified 4-F, a classification that made me untouchable. My pal Steve Rhodes also got a safe reclassification, but I can't remember why. I confess I had and still have some guilt because my brothers were getting killed in large numbers and I skated through for something silly like my height. Funny thing is, the height limit was changed to six foot eight within a year, but my 4-F kept me safe. I felt blessed and now had the obligation to do all I could to stop the war.

The other trouble I fell into was with the law. I have Detective Love to thank for that—and for the major life decision that came after. The detective hated us. Me especially. My orange-and-purple '63 Corvair with California plates was stopped and searched often. Love walked up to me during the concert with the Grateful Dead in Washington Park and said, "I'm not questioning your being here. I'm just questioning your total existence." And I responded with something like, "Wow, that's pretty good for a cop." That pissed him off.

About six months later the cops showed up at my house and arrested me for a bad twelve-dollar check. (It was a misunderstanding: I had written a check from an account I'd forgotten I'd closed.) And they didn't just arrest me; they searched the house for drugs. They didn't find anything. With Love on my back, we were extra careful.

I was thrown into jail on a Friday night, which is what cops do all the time so that you have to stay behind bars all weekend since the judges aren't available. The Supreme Court had not established the right to counsel and a speedy trial yet. So in those days you really didn't know how long you'd be in there.

I knew Love had to be behind it all. And I knew that if I wanted, I could get out right away. The woman I was dating, Audrey Hillman, came from a wealthy family in Pittsburgh. She and her parents were very involved in politics and were personal friends with a US senator in Colorado. I knew they'd have me out in five minutes. And I knew there'd be a stink about it.

I'm not sure why, but I didn't ask for Audrey's help, even though my band had a show that night. I ended up staying in jail for two or three days. It's a very powerful experience.

The first time you hear a jail door slam, you know: they're in charge; you're not. And I smelled for the first time the distinct odor of jails: a combination of sweat, Lysol, strong coffee, and, in those days, cigarettes.

I was placed in a large cell without enough room or beds for the twenty or thirty cellmates. The inmates were, as always, mostly black and Hispanic, and I was one of three or four "fish"—new, white-boy longhairs. After my shaking and sweating stopped I looked around and got really pissed. I was in jail for no reason, and most of my cellmates were in jail because they were poor and minorities. Many of them had been in for days or weeks and didn't know why. I thought, *These people are completely getting taken advantage of by the system.* I listened to their stories and learned how to roll a joint with one hand from a friendly Hells Angel.

I was released on Monday, but the damage was done. I had decided there in my cell: I would fight injustice for the rest of my life. The bounced check charges were dropped, and I quit the band shortly after that and started looking into law schools.

Audrey and I got closer. We moved in together and got engaged. I truly loved her and her family. And they loved me. The Hillmans had my life planned out: Audrey and I were going to get married and live in a mansion they would buy for us. I would attend the Wharton School for business after law school and work for the Hillmans' friends, either John Lindsay or Nelson Rockefeller. And then I'd help run the family business and/or be in politics. There was no question: that's what I was going to do. And they were so nice about it. My dad loved the idea.

5

THE SPIRO AGNEW ACID TEST

The cab driver shot me a look in the rearview mirror. "Are you crazy?" he asked. "I'm not taking you to Fourteenth and U. I don't drive there." My new address, according to the cabbie, was in a dodgy neighborhood, a neighborhood recently dubbed the most murderous in the nation. How the hell was I supposed to know? I'd found the one-room basement apartment via the *Washington Post* classifieds at the Stanford University library and sent a deposit, sight unseen. We pulled out of Dulles International Airport, and despite his protest the driver pointed the taxi toward central DC. We sped through the suburbs of Virginia, crossed a bridge over the Potomac River, and followed a bend in the road to the right. The Washington Monument swung into view on our left. I couldn't believe I was here.

Just a month earlier I'd been at a party at the home of Audrey's uncle Toby Hilliard in California, a big-ass house in Woodside, just above Menlo Park. He was a Texas oilman, a personal friend of George H. W. Bush, and just two years away from cofounding the first pro soccer team in Northern California. I mean, Toby had money. A painting by Jamie Wyeth, son of Andrew Wyeth, sat on the mantle. An *original* Jamie Wyeth. Toward the end of the party, in Toby's library, I got into a conversation with a sixty-year-old attorney and law professor. We'd both had a lot to drink. Above us, in the painting, a man wore a headlamp and carefully plucked one of three dozen mushrooms that had burst from the soil; they glowed, bulbous and ambitious in the lamplight. The lawyer asked me, in a voice that sounded like Walter Cronkite gargling gravel, "Where you going to law school?" I told him I'd soon be enrolled at UC Santa Clara. "Ah shit, man, you should go to law school in Washington, DC." he said. I think he'd gone to Georgetown or something. "You *really* need to go to law school in DC, because there's lots going on. And lots of women." I stared into the headlamp in the painting.

What can I say? The lawyer had me figured out. Within a couple days I was on the phone with the admissions offices at Georgetown, George Washington, Antioch, and Howard. They all thought I was nuts. School was starting in a few weeks. There was no way I was getting in for the 1968–69 academic year. But when I called American University, for some reason the director of admissions, Robert Goostree—who'd later do a brief stint as dean of the law school—took my call. I indicated that I was set to go to UC Santa Clara but that I had my doubts. "Oh hell," he said, "if you got in there, you can get in here, and we could use a real westerner. Come on out."

Now here I was, in the back of a cab, the National Mall scrolling to my left. We booked it along I-695, cut over to Pennsylvania Avenue, crossed the Sousa Bridge, and dropped into central DC.

It was even worse than the driver had led me to believe. We inched down Fourteenth Street in the late afternoon heat. I gagged on the stench of garbage. Rats zagged down a mountain of curbside refuse. Rusted-out cars with smashed windows flanked us on both sides; some of them had been torched. I later learned that the intersection of Fourteenth and U Street had been the site of some of the greatest unrest during the riots following the assassination of Martin Luther King Jr. in April 1968. Now, five months later, the neighborhood still looked like a revolt had torn through it. It was like a war zone in Beirut. We rolled up to the house where the basement apartment was. The driver let the cab idle.

I chickened out. "Take me to the Y," I said. So he drove me to the YMCA, where I spent the night. The next morning I visited the housing office at American University. Bad news. Since school was about to start, all the apartments and dorm rooms were full. Tacked to the community board, though, I found an ad: two women, employees at the French embassy, had a room available in exchange for a student willing to watch their kids from 3:00 PM to 6:00 PM every weekday.

I called, made an appointment to be interviewed, and we met at a café. The women were in their late thirties with one child each, a seven-year-old girl and an eight-year-old boy. They showed me the house—just across the Maryland state line and within two miles of the law school—and I was offered the job the next day.

I built a small room for myself in the basement, learned to enjoy the kids, and was spoiled by the single moms. They'd bring me coffee and French pastries in the morning on silver trays with fresh flowers. I did what I could to help out, and they were kind and supportive and even gave me a small salary in addition to room and board.

Another perk: I got invited to embassy parties. Within weeks I became a regular on the DC party circuit. Sheathed in a secondhand tuxedo, I faked my way deep into the Beltway elite. I was still engaged to Audrey Hillman but would go on more or less platonic dates with Jacqueline Kennedy's niece Eve Auchincloss and Eldie Acheson, granddaughter of Dean Acheson, the secretary of state under Truman.

The lines were blurred. At one party a guy sporting a Young Republicans button offered me a joint. Ideology seemed to have very little to do with these events. Which at the time was fine by me. My heroes were dead. When Martin Luther King was assassinated, followed by Robert Kennedy two months later, I withdrew from politics, just as I had after the death of JFK. It was too painful. I put the movement I'd championed in Denver behind me. So much easier to chase the caviar with another flute of champagne and flirt with that admiral's daughter poised at the other end of the ballroom.

But slowly, incrementally, as the months ticked by, things began to change again. The more I got to know the people running the country, the more I realized, frankly, that we were all in trouble. You'd always hear "Well, they know better." Fuck—they were idiots. Complete idiots. And many of them corrupt. I heard someone recently refer to the Nixon White House as organized crime. And it really was. Seeing that first-hand radicalized me anew.

I lived with the French women for nine months before moving into a small carriage house in Georgetown, right behind the French Market, where senators' wives bought baguettes, and across from a fire station, the sirens of which blasted at least once a night. To reflect my slow but steady return to radicalism, and with the inspiration of some good weed, I tie-dyed my entire apartment—the curtains, bedspread, sheets, and towels. It was an eyesore, but it was my eyesore.

Also around this time, in the summer of 1969, I visited the employment board at school and spotted a flyer that announced ABC News was looking for a page to work at its television studio on M Street. I applied and got the job, which involved a six-hour shift on Saturdays showing big shots around the studio, answering phones, and doing "rip and reads" of the national and international news from the teletype, and on Sundays, during another six-hour stint, setting up guests in the greenroom for *Issues and Answers*, ABC's version of *Meet the Press*, which at the moment enjoyed higher ratings than the NBC program.

The cast of characters who streamed through the doors was like the dramatis personae of the late 1960s Beltway: Ralph Nader, Spiro Agnew, Gerald Ford, George Wallace, Strom Thurmond. In fact I would eventually meet everyone of note in the Nixon White House except Nixon himself.

And because I sometimes had to pick up photos and other materials from 1600 Pennsylvania Avenue, I had White House media credentials. Yes, they gave White House credentials to a twenty-three-year-old, pot-smoking, long-haired lefty, a lefty who'd helped Jimi Hendrix score heroin just two years earlier.

The studio issued me a blue blazer—the ABC logo covered the left breast pocket—into which I tucked my midback-length ponytail. I'd walk the politicians through the studio hallways and to the greenroom, where, at 10:00 AM, I'd make them a cocktail.

One of my first guests was George Wallace, the segregationist governor of Alabama and four-time presidential candidate. He always showed up with this strange handler, whom he called the Major or something like that. The governor was often drunk before I even mixed his morning highball. I remember one Sunday, leading him and the Major through the studio, when the governor stopped at a picture window that framed M Street. A nice-looking interracial couple strolled by, hand in hand. Governor Wallace: "Look at those two niggers!" I think he was the most disgusting person I've ever met.

On the other hand, I really hit it off with the producer of *Issues and Answers*, Peggy Wheaton. She was dynamic and smart, and she encouraged me to participate in the show, even when it pissed off guests like Strom Thurmond, the pro-segregation senator from South Carolina. At an ABC-sponsored party at a hotel one night, Thurmond had wandered off, so I was dispatched to find him. I tracked him down and lightly tapped his shoulder. He was drunk and he lost it, started screaming something about me assaulting him. It didn't help that my ponytail had slipped out from my blazer. Peggy came along, and he snarled, "That long-haired fucking freak!" That's how he talked.

"Ah, Strom," Peggy said, "calm down. John will make you another drink." And he quieted down.

John Mitchell, Nixon's attorney general, three years away from serving prison time for his involvement in Watergate, hated me too. Same with Spiro Agnew, the vice president. The feeling was mutual.

See, my dive back into radicalism corresponded with the last death rattles of Americans' acceptance of the war in Vietnam. It's hard to believe in these days of apathy that there were two massive demonstrations in DC that hastened the end of the war. I was involved in the planning of both. In October 1969 there was the Moratorium, believed to be the largest protest event in history—more than two million people demonstrated nationally and in Europe. There were at least five hundred thousand in DC alone. My law school friends and I formed legal teams and security groups to keep order, and it worked: thousands were arrested, but no one was detained long. (I felt a personal triumph when Leo Seligson, one of my dad's best friends, who was rich, conservative, and generally disgusted with my long hair and antiwar attitudes, materialized at the protest and yelled at the police to stop hitting a protestor. Leo then joined us and later crowded into the office of Idaho senator Frank Church to express opposition to the war. Thereafter Leo became active in the antiwar movement and, an emotional guy, would cry at hearing the weekly body counts.)

The next month saw the Mobilization in DC, with three to four hundred thousand demonstrators. Again, my friends and I were heavily involved, securing permits and planning logistics alongside students from New York University and Columbia (they didn't know DC, but we did). Six students from Kent

State, still stunned at the murder of kids on their campus at the hands of the National Guard, crashed at my Georgetown apartment; one of them wore a helmet on which she'd painted KILL THE PIGS.

A classmate of mine, interning for John Mitchell at the Justice Department, told me that Mitchell, tobacco pipe in hand, had looked down at the thousands surrounding the building, turned to his staff, and said, "Arrest them all."

Somehow my friend and future law partner Allen Ressler and I escaped capture. We zoomed through the back alleys on his 50cc motor scooter, dodging the police and National Guard, and made it to the courthouse. Armed with intern certificates from the DC Bar Association, we ran down to the holding cells in the basement and brought five to ten people up at a time to stand before the friendly judges who would release them. We did this for more than twenty-four hours. One guy, stuffed with thirty or forty other people in a holding cell designed for five, stood holding an umbrella and sported a bowler and a three-piece suit. He looked like a banker—because he was. His name was Chester, and he was outraged. He told me the police had no regard for who they were arresting and had scooped him up. Now he wanted to be the "last person" released and take the matter to the Supreme Court. He said he was a lifelong Republican, but no more. He argued with the judge not to be released and to speak with some high-ranking Justice Department official he knew. The judge released him anyway. But this was a true transformation. Chester would never be the same.

Now, weeks later, here was the vice president sitting in the ABC greenroom. My greenroom. Agnew resembled an oversized big toe. His face had no angles. A former Democrat who had switched parties early in his political career, Agnew was governor of Maryland before becoming Nixon's right-hand man. As VP he was prone to alliterative name-calling. ("Nattering nabobs" he called my fellow war protesters and me once; another time we were "pusillanimous pussyfooters.") Four days after the Moratorium march, at a Republican fund-raiser in New Orleans, he told his donors that our struggle for peace was nothing more than the work of "an effete corps of impudent snobs."

Those words kept ringing in my head, goading me to make my move. I had come prepared. I'd known for at least a week that Agnew would be in my crosshairs. And so I'd brought a tab of LSD to the studio. It was in my pants pocket. As I slowly prepared Agnew's Manhattan, I awaited my chance. He was scheduled to go on the air in forty minutes. If I dosed the drink now and gave it to him, the acid would take hold at just the right time.

I wasn't above crossing the line with these people. On another occasion Gerald Ford, then the House minority leader, left his briefcase open in the greenroom. Inside I saw a file from the FBI labeled "top secret." Ford was not the brightest bulb on the porch. He pandered to the right wing with a crusade to impeach William O. Douglas, ostensibly on the basis of the Supreme Court justice's supposed ties to a casino financier. But what Ford really seemed focused on was that Justice Douglas was "too liberal" and was sullying the nation's morals because he'd been married so many times. I was a huge Douglas supporter, and as it happened, Cathy, his wife at the time, was my classmate and friend at law school. So I was ecstatic to discover that the classified FBI brief outlined the bureau's investigation of Douglas and that it concluded there was no legal basis to impeach, let alone begin an impeachment process. The next day I told Cathy to relax and to tell Bill to relax. I don't think she had a clue what I was talking about. Ford later dropped the investigation and became vice president.

And now the current VP was about to go on a little trip. I imagined Agnew drinking his LSD-laced cocktail, all the while silently condemning me, a bona fide hippie, for the duration of his wait in the greenroom. And then, around the time I'd be leading him out of the room and to the stage, his world would cave in. Maybe the olive green walls would undulate. Host Howard K. Smith would turn into a large reptile. The national audience would see the man undergo a psychotic breakdown. I didn't care. Agnew and his ilk had framed the policy disagreement over Vietnam as a war between conservatives and liberals, and he had resorted to name-calling. "What do you think of the effete corps *now*, Spiro?" I might ask as he blinked back, his pupils the size of pennies.

I mixed the cocktail, and it perspired on the bar. All that was left was one ingredient. I fumbled for the LSD tab in my pocket. I had to think this through. First, it wouldn't take investigators long to figure out who had done this: the longhair who prepared a cocktail for the vice president. And it would mean prison. Maybe for life. The narrative could so easily be spun to seem as if I had *poisoned* Agnew. Second, the studio could also be found culpable, particularly Peggy, who'd shown so much faith in me. I wasn't sure I was willing to see her take the fall too.

Still, it was a good idea. Agnew deserved it. I watched the clock. The window in which I had to act was closing quickly. I figured I had one more minute before the plan had to be scrapped. I pulled the tab out of my pocket. The Big Toe sat at a table, going over some notes, unaware. Thirty seconds. *Impudent snobs*, he'd called us. He still wasn't looking in my direction. No one was. All we wanted was peace. Twenty seconds. Some respect. Ten. This was my chance. Six, five, four . . .

I handed Agnew his drink. I swear he looked right into it. We both did. He tipped it back and drained the cocktail. Minutes later he was on live television, completely in control. Telling more lies. Alone backstage, I sighed, half relieved and half disappointed that I hadn't gone through with my plan. Agnew, it seemed, would go unpunished, and, worse, I feared the world would never know that he was a bad guy.

Here's the thing though. Four years later, like so many members of the Nixon administration, Spiro Agnew left the White House a disgrace. In the summer of 1973 the vice president was charged with extortion, bribery, and tax evasion connected to his time as governor. To avoid prison, he pled no contest, received three years' probation, and exited the national stage in shame, hardly to be heard from again.

Looking back, I'm glad I didn't send Agnew on an acid trip. Honestly, I'd probably still be rotting in a cell in Leavenworth today. It was also an important lesson in control. I had had the impulse to deliver my own justice. Overcoming that impulse was a huge step in my understanding of life and becoming an adult, yes, but also in my understanding of the system, a system I had vowed to fight—but of which I was becoming a part.

6

DEBORAH

The more time I spent in DC, and the more I knew what kind of lawyer I wanted to be—the kind who fought the injustices I witnessed during the marches on Washington—the more claustrophobic the Hillman family plan made me. I loved Audrey, but I didn't want my life scripted for me. I didn't want to be a corporate lawyer. And I sure as hell didn't want to be a politician.

Audrey visited me in DC frequently—she was in Pittsburgh—and with each visit the feeling nagged at me more. In the end I did the ungentlemanly thing and broke it off on the phone.

Without her in my life, I needed to connect with my closest friends more than ever, and I made frequent trips to San Francisco. Michael was there, thriving in the Bay Area music scene.

The Crystal Palace Guard had disbanded, but he was teaching guitar lessons to soon-to-be guitar greats William "Willie" Ackerman and Alex de Grassi. I also reconnected with Punky, my pal from Palo Alto High, who was in grad school at UC Berkeley. She had attended Smith College in Massachusetts before, and her roommate in the Bay Area was a Smith classmate, Deborah Beeler from Philadelphia. Like Audrey, Debbie came from an upper-class family, and she was just as pretty, with brown eyes and long brown hair she parted down the middle. The night we met we stayed up talking until 4:00 AM on Punky's couch. We talked a lot about the war, which was getting worse, the body counts rising. And we talked about prisoners' rights, something we were both passionate about. We also learned we were both vehemently against the death penalty. We clicked mentally, politically, and physically. She was working on a master's degree in English education and was so easy to talk to and so smart—intellectual in a way that no other girlfriend I'd ever had was.

She lived in Haight-Ashbury, which in 1969 was the red-hot center of the hippie universe. I started to stay at her apartment, and we'd walked up and down the street, taking it all in. I was struck by her kindness toward strangers. If we came across a homeless man, she would stop and engage him in conversation. And if she had spare change, she would hand it over. It was almost alarming how open she was, how trusting. At Christmas she joined me for a holiday party at my parents' house. I have a photo from that party that my dad took of her sitting on my lap.

I returned to DC, and we maintained a long-distance relationship, talking on the phone, occasionally exchanging letters.

When Debbie came out east to see her family, we connected in her hometown of Philadelphia. I met her parents, John and Elizabeth, who had a beautiful home in the tony neighborhood of Chestnut Hill. John, like my father, was an engineer, and was president of Precision Tool Company.

Debbie and I talked a lot on that trip about what we wanted out of our relationship. We weren't anywhere near where Audrey and I had been. We weren't ready to get engaged, but we knew we loved being around each other, even if we had lives on separate coasts. She was excited about the intern program to which she'd been accepted, teaching English at Oakland Technical High School. And I was excited about a new program I'd just started with my law school pal Allen Ressler in DC.

7

A TOTAL ECLIPSE OF THE SUN

Inspired in part by the arrests and incarcerations we'd witnessed during the Moratorium and Mobilization marches, Allen and I decided to form Law-Core, a university-based prisoners' rights project. We found a supportive mentor in Professor Nicholas Kittrie, and I wrote a grant proposal and got the funding.

We focused on three facilities: Lorton Reformatory prison in Virginia; the DC jail; and Saint Elizabeths mental hospital. We'd go in, sit with the prisoners, and help them, pro bono, with any legal help they needed. I'll admit, Lorton, the maximum-security prison for the DC area, was a scary place. But we had free roam of the facility, and I learned a lot from the prisoners, who were mostly African American. Most glaringly, it was clearer to me than ever that America's criminal justice system was based on class and race. One hardly ever saw white, middle-class people in these prisons. The black inmates I met with had grown up in inner cities, which they had never once left their entire lives. They had never seen a mountaintop. Or even a cow.

I became good friends with one Lorton inmate, Jasper, whom I was helping with a detainer issue. Jasper carried and bounced a basketball at all times and was full of wisdom, some of which, later in life, I wish I'd paid more attention to.

"John, ever tried cocaine?" he asked.

"No."

"Don't. You will like it too much."

On some nights I'd call Deborah and tell her about the work I was doing. She was proud of me. She had started to volunteer at a halfway house, teaching ex-cons how to write, and had recently moved into a cottage in the hills above Berkeley. The phone calls kept me tethered to the Bay Area.

I told her about Father Ray, a Catholic priest who oversaw the shelter near the DC jail for the families of inmates. I was at the jail two days a week, Tuesday and Thursday—quite the contrast from the weekend, when I was still rubbing shoulders with elites at ABC. Father Ray was a wonderful, just, and compassionate man, and I learned a lot from him.

The warden, not so much. I remember one chilling day when the warden showed me the electric chair DC used to execute people. Electrodes sprung from a leather biker-type beanie that they put on the condemned men's heads. Written inside the beanie were all the names of the people executed in that chair.

"Want to try it on?" the warden asked with a grin.

Absolutely not. I was against the death penalty, and he knew it. What an asshole.

I also loved telling Debbie about my life at American University. My law school was started in the mid-1880s as the Washington College of Law and was the first law school to admit women. But when I entered there were only three women in my class of about 125 students. I remember a male student telling one of the female students she was just "taking up space." He had gone to prep schools and had never been in school with women.

Sometimes I wouldn't hear from Debbie for a week or more, or I wouldn't call her. Our lives were both so busy. So I thought nothing of it in late February when I didn't hear from her for several days.

On Thursday morning, February 26, 1970, around 2:00 AM, the phone in my Georgetown cottage rang. I'd been in a deep sleep, and there were only so many people who'd call me at that hour. *Has to be Debbie*, I thought.

It was my dad. He had really bad news, he said. He was at home in Palo Alto and was holding that day's newspaper. Deborah Beeler had been found dead, lying facedown on the living room floor of her Berkeley cottage.

My whole body went cold. "Police said an electrical cord was looped several times around the neck," my dad read to me from the *Oakland Tribune*. "Death was caused by strangulation, but there were indications she was struck on the side of the head. She had been dead for at least twenty-four hours."

Because she was found wearing a short nightgown and "a slipover housecoat" and there were no signs of a forced entry or struggle, police believed she knew and trusted her assailant and likely let the person into the cottage willingly. There was no sign of a sexual assault.

I held the phone, saying nothing.

"John?" my dad said. "John, I'm sorry."

I told him I would call him later. At twenty-three I'd never had anyone that close to me die before. Over the next few days my shock hardened into anger. How could anyone hurt Debbie? I thought about her open, trusting nature, and realized that the cops could be right. Her killer was probably someone she knew. Or someone who had gained her trust quickly, not much of a challenge when it came to Debbie.

I tried to imagine her murderer. Was it one of the men at the halfway house where she volunteered? Or a stranger she had tried to help? I wanted to kill him. *If they catch this guy, I hope they electrocute his ass.* I thought those words and surprised myself. Suddenly I was considering the death penalty a good option. Because if anyone deserved it, it was the person who killed Debbie.

I fell into a deep depression. I didn't leave my apartment. Didn't eat. Didn't answer the phone. I missed classes. I was confused and heartbroken.

Finally, my friend Brad, whom I met at the University of Denver, and his girlfriend Michelle got through to me. They wanted me to visit them in Connecticut over the weekend and observe the coming solar eclipse—an eclipse the *New York Times* had billed "by far the most dramatic of the century." The plan was to take some drugs, sit on the beach, and contemplate the cosmos. Did I want to join?

On Saturday, March 7, 1970, less than two weeks after Debbie's murder, I piled into my Fiat 850, bound for Connecticut.

An eclipse! It spoke to my love of shadows, I thought, and would be a good distraction.

I spun north up I-95 with a glove compartment full of mescaline. My car *looked* like it probably contained a glove compartment full of mescaline. Painted green, the Fiat had California plates, flower stickers, antiwar stickers, and a bumper sticker that read JERRY GARCIA FOR PRESIDENT. My hair fell to the middle of my back, and I wore a red bandana for a headband.

Around Elizabeth, New Jersey, I saw red lights in my rearview mirror. The New Jersey State Patrol. I asked the trooper why he had stopped me, and he said honestly, because I was a "longhair from California and probably carrying drugs."

He started to search the car, uninvited, pulled back the driver's seat, and spotted my law books. He asked why I had them, and I told him I was a law student at American University and he had no right to search my car. He backed off, never looking in the glove compartment, and let me go on my way.

(Incidentally, my friend Allen and a few others were stopped that same weekend on the same stretch of interstate, for no reason other than their looks. We compared stories and contacted the Center for Constitutional Rights at Rutgers University Law School. A few years later I flew to New Jersey to testify in federal court, and we won. The judge issued a permanent injunction against the state police to prevent such arbitrary stops and searches.)

Brad, Michelle, and I arrived at the beach in Connecticut, only to find the sky overcast. Not exactly eclipse-viewing weather. No matter. We ingested the mescaline and roamed the shore. As the drugs took hold the Atlantic began to undulate.

It was like a giant, flat monster awaking from a long slumber. The hours blended into each other, and I remember very little about the actual eclipse or what we could see of it.

But I do remember wandering up from the beach back to the parking lot, where we saw a pile of leaves skittering across the asphalt like crabs. This fascinated us. We surrounded the pile so it would stay in place. With a piece of chalk, either Brad or Michelle or both drew a leaf identical to the leaves in the pile. Next to that they drew a double helix that snaked along the asphalt. Next to that an asterisk. These symbols meant something to Brad and Michelle, either as part of a secret language between them or as something they discovered on their mescaline trip.

They handed me the chalk. I wasn't half the artist they both were. But I drew exactly what was on my mind.

I made the line of her thin body first. From there forked two skinny legs. And tiny arms. A circle for a head. And then Debbie's long hair, parted at the middle and falling farther than it did in real life, down to her feet. Two eyes, eyebrows, a nose. For her mouth I settled on a smile, a sideways parenthesis that was a far cry from the one I'd seen on her face the last time we'd been together.

I kept going. I thought of her compassion. How she was always trying to help others. I thought about how encouraging she was of me. And I thought of the sky above and the greatest shadow caster of all, the Earth, the penumbra of which had just slid across that big ball of flame.

Below Deborah Beeler I wrote, "Try for the Sun."

8

CHICAGO

As I approached graduation my mentor, Professor Nicholas Kittrie, supported my effort to get a Ford Foundation fellowship at Northwestern University School of Law in Chicago. The fellowship focused on training grads to become *real* prosecutors or defense lawyers, since law school did nothing to prepare you for the courtroom, which was and is still true.

It was competitive and exclusive. My chances were slim. This was to be the last year of the program, and they had limited funding, only enough for two students out of more than five hundred applications. With Professor Kittrie's support, I applied and was turned down. My fallback wasn't bad though. I'd been offered a job with Kennedy and Ryan in San Francisco, the most "radical" and successful criminal law firm in the city. They were at the time representing Timothy Leary, who was living as a fugitive in Algeria. They had a cool Victorian house as their offices. I left DC in my Fiat, destination San Francisco, with a stop in Denver to visit friends.

While I was in Colorado my dad somehow tracked me down and told me over the phone that Northwestern had called and said one of the chosen fellows had opted out of the program and the grant was mine if I could be in Chicago by next Monday. It was Thursday. I was thrilled, called Kennedy and Ryan, and begged their forgiveness. They knew of the program and understood my interest in taking advantage of this special opportunity.

I arrived in Chicago late Sunday night, not knowing a soul. The law school was downtown near beautiful Lake Shore Drive and the federal courthouse. The other person who scored a fellowship was a guy named Jack Welch, from Washington State. He was just barely over five feet tall. Jurors would later laugh at us when we stood next to each other in court.

First we had to pass the Illinois bar exam, known to be one of the most difficult in the United States. I'm a bad test taker and was certain I'd fail. The bar review course was six days a week, six hours a day, and taught by some of the best legal minds in the country. The famous constitutional law professor Laurence Tribe covered constitutional and criminal laws. He was brilliant and inspiring.

Around this time I had one of the more unusual experiences in my life. Remember, after Deborah Beeler's death I had come to question my opposition to the death penalty. And I was still on the fence. Academically, I could say I was against capital punishment, but really I still wanted to see Debbie's killer in front of a firing squad.

One night I had a powerful dream. In it Debbie came to me, alive and vivid. She told me that I had to forgive rather than dishonor her death by believing in something she despised. I woke up crying and looking for her. She seemed so real. From that moment forward I vowed to honor her short life by trying to save others from the death penalty.

It was all the more incentive to study my ass off for the bar. I hit the books four or five hours a day. After two months I was burned out, and when all the information got muddled in my brain I kind of gave up. There was a Grateful Dead show the night before the bar exam, and I figured, *Why the hell not?* A friend made special brownies.

The concert ended at 2:00 AM. The bar exam started at 8:30 AM. But I was so mellowed by the night before, I eased into the three-day exam—and passed.

The administrators of the fellowship program placed Jack and me with the best criminal defense lawyers in Chicago—fabulous attorneys who were successful, demanding, and patient with us. Warren Wolfson handled high-profile organized crime cases, white-collar criminal allegations in federal court, and murder cases in state court. (His wife, Joanne, also a nationally recognized attorney, appeared on the cover of a national magazine with the cover line "I never met a murderer I didn't like.") Skip Andrew was very serious and brilliant but difficult to work for. He focused on political defendants, including the Black Panthers. (He was Panthers leader Fred Hampton's lawyer before the Chicago police murdered Fred.) Sherman Magidson was the funniest of the lot and was extra generous with his time and money. He also wrote scripts for the legal scenes in LA soap operas.

We all worked late hours, every night, at least until nine. We would go out for dinner at local mafia-type restaurants and be treated like kings. Sherman would always pay. He carried rolls of hundred-dollar bills. Jack and I were poor, living on our grant money, $600 per month. All the lawyers padded our income with food and drink, but none quite like Sherman.

In addition to working on office cases for all three lawyers, Jack and I were given our own cases, one at a time, and our mentors walked us through them point by point. Imagine the luxury. Most young lawyers starting out as prosecutors or public defenders must take on fifty files with little or no supervision. I remember asking lots of stupid questions and always getting a kind and patient reply.

The talk of Chicago police and judicial corruption were more than rumors, I came to learn. Sometimes it was funny. The first case I had on my own involved a young black man, a "manager" of women of the night, charged with a petty drug offense. His name was Prince Albert McManus, and he wore a red velvet cape.

This was in the infamous drug court at the criminal courts building at Twenty-Sixth and California, where a testy old judge disposed twenty or thirty cases a day. I wrote a brief for Prince and filed a motion to suppress because of an illegal arrest and search. The judge tossed the brief back at me and said, "We don't use these things here, boy. Go out in the hall and talk to the district attorney or a cop."

Stunned, I exited the courtroom with Prince. In the hallway a man said, "Pssst, come here." He was the arresting officer and said for $500 he would "change" his testimony. What was my ethical response?

"I don't have $500."

Prince negotiated directly with the cop, and they reached some kind of understanding. The case was dismissed. Prince laughed at my naïveté but thanked me for my hard work. (He later died in a shoot-out with some Blackstone Ranger gang members.)

I got another glimpse of the corruption when Warren sent me alone to cover some small pretrial matter in a homicide case. I had just started working for him and was pumped about being in a real court for a murder trial. I arrived at 8:30 AM, ready for my case to be called, and waited—and waited. There were a lot of cases on the docket but not *that* many. Around 11:00 the judge announced a lunch break. I was the only lawyer left in the pews.

I went across the street, had some lunch, then visited my client in the holding cell. He asked what was taking so long, and I told him I didn't know. He then asked me if I'd paid the bribe. "*The what?*" He laughed and said to go find a public defender to explain the situation to me. I did and was informed that the judge would not call my case until money was paid to the clerk! All the lawyers did it, or you would get nothing done on your cases. You'd walk up to the clerk and ask for the file on, say, *State v. Smith*. He'd hand you the court file, you'd pretend to look at it, fold cash up in your hand, and pass the file and the money back to the clerk. In those days if you were a public defender, the cost was three dollars. A private attorney paid five. (I only paid three. They knew I was a poor student.) I went back to the office, and the lawyers all laughed at me because I was in court almost all day before I figured out the system.

On another occasion my naïveté cost Warren $500. It was common knowledge that prosecutors, police, and judges in the city could be bought, but Warren and the others in our office never played the game. Sure, five bucks to a clerk to avoid waiting all day was one thing, but they steered clear of the deeper corruption. And ignorance on my part almost got me fired for unknowingly participating.

In all murder cases in Illinois there were coroners' inquests that determined the cause and manner of death (murder, suicide, natural causes, etc.). The results were not binding but could influence a prosecutor's decision to charge murder or manslaughter. The inquest result was up for purchase, but again, our office never participated in that kind of graft.

Warren sent me alone to do an inquest for one of our clients. This was a big deal, a mini-trial of sorts, questioning witnesses and making objections in a potential murder case. After the hearing the detective in the case walked up to me in the hall and gave me a large manila envelope containing all the police reports, the "discovery." I said, "Uh, thanks," and was surprised, as I knew it wasn't required by law at the time that I be provided with the discovery. I went back to the office and was excited to tell Warren this nice cop gave me the entire discovery.

"You asshole," he said. "You just cost me $500." He was more concerned about violating our no-graft policy than the money.

I learned a great deal from the kind, generous, and talented attorneys I worked for. I sat second chair in a few trials with Warren. He never lost. And I did a few cases by myself and some with Jack. Jack and I even had a federal case in front of the infamous Judge Julius Hoffman, of Chicago Seven fame. He hated me, my long hair, and my refusal to cater to his judicial arrogance. He was also intimidated by my height. He was a small man with a small-man complex. He sent me home to change clothes one day because my suit was brown, not black or blue as required. We reached a plea agreement during trial to end the agony.

There were parts of Chicago I loved: the music scene, my neighborhood (the Near North Side), the food, the museums, and the places and events that were just plain unique. The famous People's Law Office was located near my apartment and full of dedicated radical lawyers. I hung out there often. On Saint Patrick's Day the Chicago River was dyed green and the judges wore green robes, except for Judge Olson, who wore a Viking helmet. No kidding. I had a preliminary hearing for a murder case in front him on Saint Paddy's Day, and he wore the helmet all day.

9

I GO TO PRISON

How to put this? I was a child molester. As far as the guards and inmates at the maximum-security penitentiary in Shelton, Washington, knew, that's what I was in for. Aside from the warden, only my boss and a member of the parole board—both of whom were also posing as prisoners—knew the truth.

My first idea as the newest assistant to the state's attorney general was to glean all I could about prison life from the inside. Back at Northwestern Law School I'd responded to a post in the placement office. Washington State sought an attorney with experience in corrections to help rewrite its rules of incarceration. I interviewed with my future boss Don Horowitz over the phone—he later confessed he initially returned my call because he thought my name, John Henry, meant I was black and the AG's office needed diversity.

A couple weeks later, in February 1972, I was on a plane bound for western Washington. From my window I could see Mount Rainier and was happy to be back on my beloved West Coast.

Asked for ideas on how to reform the state's prisons, I said, "Let's go to one."

So in July a representative from the parole board, Don, and I were cuffed, placed in a van, and driven out to Shelton prison, where we planned to spend the week. We got to choose our own fake crimes. I went with child rape because I wanted to experience the most extreme treatment. Prisoners hate pedophiles.

I got in trouble the first night. I had to take a shit, but my toilet was visible from a catwalk in the cellblock. So I unscrewed the lightbulb hanging from the ceiling, to make it dark. A guard ran up screaming. Tampering with the lights was a violation, and I was punished with the loss of outdoor privileges for two days—no notice, no hearing, no due process.

I was one of the few white prisoners in my cellblock and learned quickly that this was not a good thing. The guy in the cell on the right was in for killing two people during a bank holdup gone wrong, and he hated me. A member of the revolutionary civil rights group the George Jackson Brigade occupied the cell on the left. His name was Marx—yes, Marx, not Mark—and he took me under his protection after he learned of my past participation in major civil rights groups in the '60s. (I later represented him in federal court for probation violation.)

After my punishment for bulb tampering was over I was allowed into the yard three hours a day and tried to remain inconspicuous. I played some basketball, lifted weights, and smoked hand-rolled cigarettes. I was a new fish who nobody liked, but many wanted me to be their "boy," in a sexual sense. With Marx's help, I avoided that particular problem.

The noise was the worst. If you imagine a large male dormitory at a college open on one side to a hall and everyone playing radios and TVs (all on different stations) as loud as possible—and yelling as loud as possible—you might get some idea of what the noise was like. The correctional officers (they'd hit you if you called them guards) were mostly country boys with little education, not too different from the inmates themselves. And some of the guards were just plain sadistic. You learn who the dangerous guards are very quickly and avoid ever being alone with them. One guard in particular was proud to be called a redneck and carried a sock full of soap bars he used to beat people without leaving obvious marks. Prison is torture.

Back in Olympia after our stay at Shelton we drafted new due process rules to control how and when prison authorities could place inmates in segregation or isolation ("the hole"). Administrators and correctional officers resisted these new rules. So I called up my old law school pal Allen Ressler, who had moved to the state to run a prison legal aid project, and told him to sue us. He did and won. Now our rules were court ordered.

The most resistance came from the administrators and officers at Washington State Penitentiary in Walla Walla, an imposing edifice constructed in the late 1800s. It was also home to Washington State's death chamber, where the state executed people by hanging. The warden, Bobby Rhay, hated me and my long hair—still halfway down my back—and took to calling me John Henry Fucking Browne. He would complain to me in writing on state letterhead and would literally start his correspondence, "Dear John Henry Fucking Browne."

I had free run of his maximum-security prison and often went to the hole and other segregation cells to look into why and how inmates were so housed. If I determined that procedures were not followed, I had the authority to demand an inmate be released from those cells, and did so often.

I began teaching correctional officers prison law at night for free. I tried to get across to them that due process was simple fairness in procedures that affect people's lives. After a year or so the officers came around and began to show greater regard for the rights of the men in their charge.

I became sort of a hero to some of the inmates and used my influence to calm ethnic tensions and potentially homicidal conflicts. The black prisoners formed an organization with my help, the Black Prisoners Forum Unlimited. I was the only white person allowed to attend their meetings. I was also involved with an inmate governance council, the RGC (resident governance council), and attended their meetings and carried their grievances to the administrators.

One of the leaders of the RGC was a fellow named Bud doing a two-year stretch for a minor offense. He asked me one day why the parole board kept preventing his release after he met with them. I told him it might have something to do with the tattoo on his forehead that said FUCK OFF. I helped get some volunteer plastic surgeons in to remove the tattoo. He was eventually paroled.

The most unique group in the prison was Lifers with Hope. To his credit, this was Warden Bobby Rhay's idea, and it was this kind of innovation that got him on the cover of *Life* magazine. Lifers often cause trouble because they have nothing to look forward to. I convinced many of them to join Rhay's Lifers with Hope, and the warden and I grew to respect each other. The lifers went to high schools and Rotary clubs and gave talks. Rhay even started a Take a Lifer to Dinner program. No kidding. Citizens would check out a lifer and take him to dinner.

I had a lot of power in this job and helped make some vital changes. It was, however, a quick burnout. Trying to change the prison system was a daunting task.

After two years I left Olympia to accept a job with the King County public defender's office in Seattle. Almost as soon as I got there, there were stories in the media about young women disappearing in and around the city.

Ted Bundy was about to enter my life.

10

THE KILLER BESIDE ME

The airplane banked, and the passenger window framed the lake below—a mammoth black body of water that seemingly stretched from horizon to horizon. They say the lake is 27 percent salt and that's what keeps it so still, like an oil slick. Beyond, to the west, lie the salt flats, blank-canvas white, racing out to meet the skyline. And to the east: the toothy Wasatch Range with its hundreds of slot canyons—canyons in which the good people of Utah said that Ted Bundy had stashed the mutilated corpses of their daughters.

I had come to the Beehive State half expecting the usual media frenzy surrounding my client. The *Salt Lake Tribune*, top of the fold, told a different story that morning, January 17, 1977: RITTER STAYS GILMORE EXECUTION AFTER LAST DITCH APPEAL. The article detailed US district court judge Willis

Ritter's latest deliberations surrounding the death-by-firing-squad execution of thirty-six-year-old Gary Gilmore, who six months earlier had murdered two men in nearby Provo and Orem.

I rolled out from Salt Lake International Airport and made my way to State Street, an extra-wide, six-lane boulevard originally made so wide, I later learned, to accommodate the horse-drawn wagons of Brigham Young's Promised Land, his City of Zion in the wilderness. I drove past countless pawnshops and gun stores. An inch of snow blanketed the sidewalk. I tried to imagine what had drawn Ted to this city, what about it had made it such an appealing place for his secret, violent life. Was it the desolation? The affability of its too-trusting people? All I got for an answer as I wheeled down State Street was Mount Olympus, a bluff of granite rising in front of me and off to the left, as if it guarded the southern end of the Salt Lake Valley. Beyond Olympus sat Utah State Prison, known locally as simply Point of the Mountain.

The prison parking lot was crowded with the clamshells of television satellite antennae. Reporters vamped in front of cameras and jawed on about Gilmore's fate for the audiences of NBC, CBS, and ABC. No one had been executed for homicide in the United States since 1967, when the Supreme Court decision *Furman v. Georgia* had deemed capital punishment unconstitutional on the grounds that it was deployed as "cruel and unusual punishment," in violation of the Eighth Amendment. The moratorium lasted almost a decade until a 1976 Supreme Court ruling, *Gregg v. Georgia*, restored the practice.

When Gilmore admitted to gunning down two men—a law student working as a gas station attendant and a motel manager—at point-blank range, a jury found him deserving of the death penalty. That put him right in the crosshairs of the State of Utah, which seemed more than willing to exercise its newfound right to end his life. His supposed death wish sped the process along. He refused to make any appeals and fired his lawyers when they tried. He also insisted that he die by firing squad rather than the relatively less barbaric method of electrocution.

Now the whirl outside the prison was merely academic. Even that morning's *Tribune* story was late to the punch. Gilmore was dead before the newspaper ink had dried.

At dawn the guards had escorted Gilmore out of his cell and behind the prison. The mercury had dropped to twenty-four degrees. He wore only a sleeveless black T-shirt, white cotton pants, and tennis shoes. They drove him into a warehouse and sat him in what had once been an office chair. Asked if he had any final words, Gilmore, before a small audience, said, "Let's do it." A physician threw a black hood over his head. Four gunmen emptied their rifles into his chest, killing him instantly.

It was an ominous situation to walk into: the death penalty was back, and my client, accused of capital offenses, sat on the other side of the penitentiary walls, just yards away from the inaugural execution of a new era. This weighed heavily on me as I was ushered into the prison—same smell of piss, sweat, and burned coffee as all the others—and down a corridor to the office in which I'd be meeting with Ted Bundy.

He was serving his one-to-fifteen-year sentence for the aggravated kidnapping of Carol DeRonch and had been charged, in October 1976, with killing Caryn Campbell in Aspen,

Colorado. He was fighting extradition to Colorado. No charges had been filed in Washington State.

A large rectangular table sat in the middle of the room. The surrounding walls were covered with the bathroom-stall-style graffiti of inmates, including that of the now deceased Gary Gilmore. I unpacked my mobile library, some of it regarding allegations against Ted in Colorado but mostly books and treatises on how to fight extradition and avoid the death penalty.

A guard led my client into the room. Ted looked like a different person nearly every time I'd seen him, and on this occasion he was thin and wiry, with short hair and a clean-shaven face. He came armed with his usual boxes of legal materials, including drafts of motions to suppress evidence and new pleadings that alleged incompetency on the part of his Utah counsel and various errors committed by trial judge Stewart Hanson.

Two things distinguished this meeting with Ted from those that had come before. For the first time since I'd begun representing him in the winter of 1976, he showed no interest in casual conversation. He didn't ask about the suit I wore. Didn't even look at my shoes. He was all business.

Second, Ted stopped being coy about the charges against him. He informed me that he was involved in the "Ted" murders in Washington State and was responsible for countless other homicides in California, Oregon, Idaho, and Utah. This was no shock, as I had for some time considered him to be exactly who the police thought he was. But to hear the man say it was another thing.

Without providing details, he began cataloging his kills for me, starting with the murder of a young woman on January 31,

1974, followed by homicides on March 12 and April 17, 1974. (I took these to be Lynda Ann Healy, Donna Manson, and Susan Rancourt, respectively.) Going through his list as if it were a résumé, he informed me the next homicide was in Oregon in May 1974 (which I assumed was that of Roberta Parks).

Next he listed the June 1, 1974, murder of a woman (Brenda Ball) he met at The Flame Tavern, a bar outside of Seattle frequented by college students but also well known as a place where homosexuals hooked up. This homicide, he said, was followed ten days later, June 11, 1974, by another (Georgeann Hawkins).

He listed two homicides on July 14, 1974, which would be Janice Ott and Denise Naslund, who went missing from Lake Sammamish State Park. He said he had a memory, but not a clear one, of killing a woman in Vancouver, Washington, a month later. (I didn't know of that victim.)

In the middle of this bizarre time line he paused to tell me that, in an effort to meet influential people in Utah, he had joined the Mormon Church in 1975, and then went on to list ten more victims, none by name but all corresponding to the dates of murders for which he was suspected.

Then out of nowhere, and almost as another aside, Ted told me that he had traveled to California in 1972 or 1973 and killed at least eight individuals during that trip. I knew these California murders, if they existed, were not on the radar of any law enforcement agency investigating him. (It would be years before I would realize just how close to home that revelation was.)

The confessions that would pour out of Ted over the next two years—again, solely to me, in dank prison rooms—would continue to shock me. But even as he confirmed what I already suspected, a feeling came over me. It clawed its way into my chest, an unholy hybrid: my sense of duty to save a man's life, fused with my absolute disgust for that man and his actions. I couldn't tell if I was angry, traumatized, or both.

I betrayed none of this to Ted. I just listened. He was concerned that Utah authorities would find more bodies and that it would be more likely, and quicker, to achieve the death penalty in Utah—with its new taste for blood—than it would be in Colorado. (Though the latter state was in the process of reinstating capital punishment, it did not at the moment have the legal machinations to put a convicted killer to death.)

The plan was to stall extradition to Colorado for only a few weeks, long enough to give Ted time to strategize and find a new lawyer in Utah and another in Colorado, and then waive extradition and go to Colorado. I told him I'd help find the right lawyers as well as deliver messages to his family and friends in Seattle.

He didn't state it explicitly, but I began to suspect by the meeting's end that Ted had a secret game plan, one that involved providing me enough information so I could ultimately assist him in returning to Washington and perhaps working out some sort of plea bargain—unlikely—that would allow him to spend the rest of his life in a mental institution there.

I collected my documents and books and shook his hand. I couldn't wait to get home. As the Seattle-bound airplane left the tarmac, the Great Salt Lake, black as ever, filled my window once again. Much of what Ted had told me was still on my mind as the g-force of the plane's rise pulled at my guts. I thought of Gilmore's execution and what it meant for my serial killer client. What it meant for my future clients—and for the kind of career I was building for myself. The gravity of it all tugged at me until the plane plateaued and the dead sea dissolved behind me.

11

ESCAPE

After meeting with him in Utah I went through a period during which I wanted nothing more to do with Ted Bundy. I waited several months and in the fall finally wrote a letter telling him I would be happy to introduce him to attorneys I knew in Denver and Aspen but was bowing out as his counsel.

It should have been apparent to him that the things he told me at Point of the Mountain had completely freaked me out, and it amazed me that he would think otherwise. On October 31, nine months after my visit to Utah State Prison, he replied to my letter with the following:

> Dear John:
>
> Thank you for your letter of October 27. I too, wish the circumstances of our first contact since last February were

different. I had intended to write to you on several occasions during the past several months to express my appreciation for the moral and professional support you have given me and my girlfriend and others close to me.

Recent developments seem to indicate that I will be desperately in need of such support in the near future. I have had a tendency to be overly analytical about the motivations of the Colorado authorities in filing their case at this time. I suppose my real concern should not be "why" they filed but "what," they filed. Whatever their reasoning, they have taken the plunge and are now committed to follow through. . . . You have no obligation to come to my aid, but I am begging you to do so because my life hangs in the balance. I am asking you to provide whatever services you can offer, because I am immensely impressed by your legal intelligence and more so because I like you and feel comfortable with you. I need your help now more than I have ever needed help before in my life. What more can I say except "please" help me?

Sincerely,

Ted

PS: I will avoid discussing details of the Colorado case in letters. I will only talk about the case directly to my present attorneys. If you should have questions, submit them through my present attorneys, and if you haven't read Colorado's affidavit, I will ask my present attorney to send you a copy, should you be in a position to help, that is.

In this letter I observed a change in Ted's personality. Always projecting a sense of control, he never begged for anything. It got my attention. I wanted out, but here was someone begging for his life. I sent back a brief reply that I would indeed help him but didn't think I could afford to without getting paid. I also told him I'd help him find good attorneys in Utah and Colorado. He wrote back right away. That letter read, in part*:

> I have written my present attorney asking his opinion on several critical matters, including extradition, and requesting a meeting with him before I go to Colorado.
>
> Of course I would prefer an alliance between my present attorney and you. If I had a choice at this moment between the two of you, I would choose you, but I am not sure I can afford that choice.
>
> I am in complete agreement concerning guaranteed reimbursement for expenses and lost salary should I ask you to handle my case. Is there any way you could give me some general estimate of what this might amount to . . . ?
>
> I will be extradited . . . no matter what, but by opposing extradition, are there advantages which outweigh the disadvantages? . . .
>
> I think it is perfectly suicidal to rush into a strange state and be represented by an unknown attorney who has but a few weeks to prepare against a case, which the prosecution has been plotting for over a year. I believe it is literally suicide. What do you recommend?

The letter omitted any mention of the lengthy confession he made to me in Utah in anticipation of some sort of psychological defense. He seemed to have slipped back into attempting to defend himself on the facts of the case. As any

* For the full text of the letters Ted Bundy sent me, see appendix B, page 223.

good attorney knows, fighting extradition is quite hopeless and will just result in negative publicity and a sense that the defendant is trying to use every trick in the book to avoid facing the ultimate trial.

More interesting are the reasons he thought extradition should be fought: to obtain more time to prepare. Ted totally ignored the solid facts present in the Aspen case. Both eyewitness identification and his credit card activity put him near the scene within hours of Caryn Campbell's disappearance.

My next letter from Ted arrived in late November and evidenced his outrage about a story that appeared in the November 24, 1976, issue of the *Seattle Times*, with the headline FBI LINKS HAIR SAMPLES TO BUNDY. The FBI had released a report that Caryn Campbell's hair and scalp samples were found on the front floor mat of Ted's VW. The article also noted that prison authorities had recently transferred Ted to the maximum-security unit "after being found with escape materials, including false identification and information on airline schedules."

> This is just not something I expected from the Times. What are they doing, warming up the cross for my crucifixion?
>
> This is one of the most flagrant examples of prosecution by the press that I have seen. The worst thing about this Seattle Times article is that it will be carried by the wire services and broadcast in the Denver and the Aspen area.
>
> Damn it, John, I can't get used to this abuse. The impact of the article is deadly, without the knowledge that hair samples are far from being identification. . . .

> Note also how the fallacious escape materials—also how the escape material allegation is injected to magnify the inferences of guilt.
>
> The intent of the article is purely malicious and prejudicial. I feel powerless as I watch my conviction firsthand by the media.

Though I paid attention to his story in the media—including his January 1977 extradition to Colorado—I lost contact with Ted after that last letter and was almost able to keep him out of my mind until I woke up on the morning of June 8, 1977, to a headline in the *Seattle Times* that read, in large print, BUNDY ESCAPES. It was accompanied by a picture of Ted sitting in the jail's law library, with leg irons on, across from an open window, which was a mere ten feet up from the ground outside.

Apparently Ted had convinced the jailers he could be trusted, and they removed his leg irons so he could walk more freely through the library. When they weren't looking he jumped out of the window, sprained his ankle when he landed, and hobbled along the nearby river. He hid out for six days in the mountains surrounding Aspen. He was apprehended coming through town in the middle of the night in a stolen car, which led me to believe he actually wanted to get caught, as he could have driven over another pass and left Aspen for good.

On June 14, the day after he was caught, I was flown out to Aspen on his parents' dime. I found Ted asleep in the basement jail cell that once belonged to Doc Holliday (there was a plaque). He was curled up on the floor with a blanket, no mattress.

The jailers banged their boots on the cell door and said, "Hey, Bundy, you've got a visitor." It took a while for Ted to wake up. When he did he looked up, saw me standing next to two guards, and said, "Hey, John, did you figure out which one of those guys pushed me out the window?"

The guards did not find this amusing. They said something rude to both of us and locked me in the cell with Ted. He and I then had one of our most fateful conversations. I had the paperwork charging him with the death penalty in Colorado. We went over the materials for a while, and then Ted asked, "John, where would a person actually go in order to obtain the death penalty?" In other words, which states actually carry out the death penalty?

I responded without hesitation, "Florida and Texas." Their statutes had recently been upheld as constitutional.

We then discussed the Colorado death penalty statute, its potential unconstitutionality, and also options he might have by returning to Washington State. He had a list of victims he was willing to admit to killing in Washington and asked whether it would be possible to return to Washington plead guilty to a number of murder charges, and obtain a life sentence, not the death penalty. I said I'd pursue this idea, but only if he seriously contemplated informing Washington State authorities of the specifics of his crimes. He told me he would think about it.

As usual he was dissatisfied with his assigned public defenders and inquired whether I could find a qualified private attorney in Colorado who would be willing to assist him. I had someone in mind. During the summer between my first and second year of law school, I had worked in Denver with a very gifted attorney named Marshall Quiet.

Although Marshall was getting on in years, I still felt he was an excellent attorney. I called and asked whether he would be willing to assist Ted. Marshall said his overhead was such that he could not afford to do a pro bono case, or even a case paid at public defender rates. However, he did remind me of a friend of his in Aspen named Stephen "Buzzy" Ware, who he thought might be interested in taking Ted's case on a pro bono or a reduced-fee basis. I was familiar with Buzzy from my band days in Aspen.

Buzzy was a fascinating individual who had long, flowing hair and drove Harley-Davidson and Triumph motorcycles way too fast. He agreed to assist Ted and become lead counsel. Unfortunately, within two weeks of this decision, Buzzy was in a motorcycle accident, which killed his beloved wife and completely incapacitated his ability to rationally put thoughts together. I thought I was off the case, but Buzzy's serious injuries meant I'd be pulled back in.

During this trip I also had some classic Aspen experiences. The town had become even more radical than when I used to come through with the Crystal Palace Guard. I was walking down the street, and a hippie type walked up to me and asked me if I was that "Ted Bundy lawyer." I responded in the affirmative, and he said, "Well, hey, man, I hope I get on that jury because, you know, murder is just relative!"

Ted was transferred to the relatively high-security jail in Glenwood Springs, Colorado, about a thirty-five-minute drive from Aspen. It was a small facility, only housing twenty or so prisoners, and Ted was watched carefully. All his mail was screened, and his phone calls were monitored.

On July 7, 1977, I received a rather unusual typewritten letter from him. He wrote:

Dear John:
Good heavens . . . it has been over three weeks since my early morning call to you upon my return to captivity, and I am just getting around to saying, quote, "thank you," to you for coming to my aid, coming to Aspen, and just generally making me feel less like a fumbling, stupid idiot I was behaving like.

Aw, but that adventurous chapter is behind me, or so I would like to think at this moment. The ghosts of my escapade will return [in] the form of five counts and a new information. I will behave like the hardened convict I am and say, quote, "Fuck it. I have got broad shoulders." That is what a hard con would say, isn't it?

Since my return, I have been in procrastination—in a procrastination inspired slump. ("I have got plenty of time; the suppression hearing isn't for two months.")

Instead of working, I have been doing push-ups, pull-ups, jumping rope, and have done my best to emulate Tarzan. I am eating nuts, took vitamins, gagged on nutritional yeast, and in the process have (at least to my own mind) become a superb physical specimen. . . .

How much is it worth to you to have me tell you that I can't imagine a finer defense attorney than yourself? It's true. I consider myself an expert on the good ones and the bad ones.

Best wishes,
Ted

Now, in retrospect, this letter from Ted should have been a clue—the new exercise routine, the diet. Shortly after receiving this letter I visited him at the Glenwood Springs jail and noticed that he had lost at least twenty pounds, perhaps more. He looked completely different.

He appeared to be in excellent shape, but I was curious as to why he had lost so much weight, as he was never heavy to begin with.

You would think the implications of his weight loss would be obvious not only to me but also to his jailers. But apparently not. You see, Ted's cell was right next to a jailer's live-in apartment, and there was a grated vent in the ceiling of his cell. The hole, approximately a square foot in size, would be impossible for any person to get through unless he was extremely fit, agile, and thin.

Ted made a series of phone calls on the night of December 30, 1977. He called Richard Larsen, a reporter at the *Seattle Times*; his friend and coworker Ann Rule; and me. I remember the phone call vividly, as I was not expecting to hear from Ted so close to New Year's Eve. The conversation was a bit strange in that it seemed to have no real purpose. He had recently won some very important victories in court.

Judge George Lohr had determined that none of the "common scheme or plan" evidence would be introduced in Ted's Colorado trial, a major victory. Furthermore, Judge Lohr had declared the Colorado death penalty statute unconstitutional. So one would think Ted would be better off remaining in Colorado than going to a state more likely to impose the death penalty.

And yet that night, hours after he called me, Ted Bundy escaped again.

He later informed me, during conversations we had in Florida, that he actually escaped one day prior to when the authorities revealed it to the public. He had obtained a detailed map of the Glenwood Springs jail and knew all the air ducts and lighting fixtures and where one could escape through the jailer's apartment.

On December 29 he placed articles in his bed to make it look like he was asleep, went to the twelve-inch vent, and slithered through the air duct and down into the closet in the jailer's apartment. He knew the jailer often left without authorization to visit a girlfriend and had done so on this night.

Because his cell had no windows, Ted didn't know he was stepping out into a Colorado blizzard that had dumped an additional six inches of snow on top of the twelve inches that had fallen the previous day. An associate had bought a car for him and left it in the parking lot with a change of clothes and a substantial amount of cash.

Unfortunately for Ted, the associate purchased an MG Midget, the world's worst car for navigating blizzard conditions in Colorado. Ted got in the Midget, changed clothes, and drove toward Vail. In between Glenwood Springs and Vail, the Midget, which had no snow tires or chains, sped into a snowbank and was completely disabled.

Ted flagged down a law enforcement officer, probably a highway patrolman, who helped pull the Midget out of the snowbank, and Ted drove to Vail, where the Midget bit the dust. He then took a bus from Vail to Denver and an airplane from Denver to Chicago. All during this time, the public was unaware that Ted Bundy had escaped, again.

He later told me he was watching the Rose Bowl in a bar in Ann Arbor, Michigan, when a newsflash came on indicating that Ted Bundy had broken out of the Glenwood Springs jail.

12

A BARGAIN

The next stage of Ted's saga seems completely unbelievable and has led me to the conclusion that Ted, all along, wanted to be caught in a dramatic fashion in a state where the death penalty was definitely going to be imposed.

Although he had a false ID and could get his hands on enough money to get by in a city where he could easily disappear, such as Chicago or Ann Arbor, he chose to travel to a college town, Tallahassee, home of Florida State University.

Ted, at thirty-one, was much older than most college students, but he still looked young and fit since losing weight and working out in the Glenwood Springs jail. He obtained an inexpensive apartment and survived by stealing wallets and purses from customers at local supermarkets. He also purchased an inexpensive bike and on occasion stole VW Bugs, his favorite mode of transportation.

Ted told me that he arrived at Florida State University on January 8, 1978, within ten days of leaving the blizzard in Glenwood Springs. Although he was on the FBI's Ten Most Wanted list, he blended well into campus life and nobody seemed to pay any attention to him.

Six days after arriving in Tallahassee he killed two college students at the Chi Omega sorority house and severely injured two others. Later on that night he brutally attacked a dance student residing in a basement apartment. She survived the life-threatening injuries. Police officials spoke to a number of witnesses from the Chi Omega sorority house, one of whom provided them with two chillingly accurate drawings of the intruder she saw, both bearing a haunting likeness to Ted Bundy.

One of the drawings captures his very distinctive nose, and the other depicts him creeping with a stocking cap into the sorority house and up the stairs with a club, later determined to be a piece of firewood.

The terrible events of this night shocked the city of Tallahassee, the entire state of Florida, and for the most part the southern United States. However, no one seemed to notice the similarities between these attacks and the attacks of women in the northwestern and western states.

I first learned of Ted's second escape from jail upon returning from a trip to Mexico. On my arrival at the airport in Seattle, the *Seattle Times* headline blared TED BUNDY ESCAPES JAIL AGAIN. I couldn't believe the authorities would allow

Bundy to escape under any circumstances, and had the chilling feeling we'd be hearing about his deadly exploits soon.

Of course, I had no idea where he would travel, and had no contact with him until February. It is still unfathomable to me that professional law enforcement and corrections officials would allow Ted to escape a second time. I would assume after his first escape that he would have been under constant observation and certainly not housed somewhere with a vent whose grate could be removed.

His first escape, I believe, was impetuous and opportunistic and involved no planning whatsoever. This second escape was well executed, with the assistance of an accomplice.

The only conclusion I can come to is that Ted used his charisma, which he utilized in obtaining the trust of countless victims over the years, to charm his keepers to the extent that they allowed him privileges and freedom within the correctional institutions not often provided to others. This, despite his previous escape and horrendous criminal charges.

If any western law enforcement officers investigating Ted had seen the composite drawings of the intruder at Chi Omega, they would have immediately recognized the intruder as Ted Bundy.

Of course we all knew that if Ted Bundy were loose, there would be more murders. There was nothing I could do to prevent further criminal behavior on Ted's part, and certainly nothing the police authorities could do since they had no idea where he was.

On February 16, 1978, at 5:00 PM I was sitting on the couch in my new office in Seattle, where I was now a full-time private attorney, going over the day's work. I received a phone call through my answering service from someone in Florida. The caller gave the name Rosebud, and I knew immediately it was Ted, trying to conceal his identity.

I accepted the phone call and had a lengthy and bizarre conversation with him. He had been detained for suspicious behavior and auto theft, but the cops had no idea who he was. On the phone he was completely insane, wandering from one subject to the next. It seemed he was either in the midst of some sort of psychotic break or under the influence of a powerful drug.

He told me he was in jail in Florida and that it was only a matter of time until they found out who he was. I agreed and suggested that he inform the authorities of his identity so it would look like he was at least being cooperative.

He made me promise not to reveal his identity until the following day. I agreed. This haunts me to this day. I knew he was in custody and therefore no longer a danger to others, but had no idea of the crimes he had committed in Florida.

I was concerned that if he were released before they determined his identity, he would kill again. So I wanted to contact law enforcement in Washington State and let them know that Ted was now in custody in Florida, but my dedication to the attorney-client privilege prevented me from doing so. I didn't sleep that night, and at one point I even dialed the Ted Task Force office, but hung up before anyone answered. I told myself that Ted, as had become his pattern, would also call Ann Rule or Richard Larsen, both of whom could ethically call the police and tell them about the nattering mystery jail inmate in Florida.

The next morning I awoke to news reports that Ted Bundy had been apprehended in Lake City, Florida, and was being investigated for crimes committed in that state since his escape from Glenwood Springs, including the murders of the sorority sisters at Chi Omega and the attack on the nearby dance student. He was also being actively investigated for the disappearance of a twelve-year-old girl, Kimberly Leach, who was missing but had not been found.

I had determined that I was finished assisting Ted in any capacity unless it was an attempt to prevent the death penalty from being imposed. I enlisted the help of Millard Farmer, a very well-respected anti–death penalty attorney from Atlanta, Georgia. He was one of the founders of the Southern Poverty Law Center and dedicated his entire career to defending those charged with death penalty offenses. Although Millard and I weren't Ted's official lawyers in the Florida cases, we worked with Ted in the hopes of arranging some sort of plea bargain that would save his sorry life.

The plea bargain would involve an agreement by Florida, Utah, Colorado, and even Washington not to prosecute Ted for any death penalty cases if he pled guilty in Florida. In my wild imagination, I could not foresee any possibility of arriving at such a plea bargain for the man who had become, at the time, the most notorious serial killer in the United States.

To my surprise, Millard and I were successful in obtaining a written plea bargain, and in May 1979 he and I spent a great deal of time with Ted at the Tallahassee jail trying to convince him to accept it. But Ted was resistant immediately to any attempt to resolve his case with a life sentence.

Millard and I knew Ted could be worn down and were hoping that we could literally deprive him of sleep to the extent that he would sign the paperwork and we could finalize the deal. I would spend four or five hours with Ted in the jail cell, and then Millard would enter and spend four or five hours with him while I went to the hotel and slept. This process went on over a period of two or three days.

My time in Tallahassee with Millard Farmer was quite extraordinary. Millard was a folk hero to many college students in this era, and we were stopped constantly by students in restaurants and even on the street, asking for autographs from Millard and information as to the progress on the attempts to save Ted's life.

Millard was always gracious and kind to anyone who wanted some of his time. I remember fondly that the thin Millard maintained his weight by drinking only Diet Coke or Diet Pepsi during the day and eating very light meals at night. When he was not working, which seemed rare, he was reading material regarding death penalty advocates and writing pamphlets on how to defend those accused of death penalty crimes.

Spending time with Millard was definitely a highlight of my career, and I will always fondly remember him as a zealous advocate for the right to life.

The magnitude of our task was overwhelming, as Florida and Texas were known as the buckle of the Death Belt in the South, where people were executed without much due process, without the aid of competent lawyers, and with very little appellate review. As I told Ted in Aspen after his first escape, "If you really want to get executed, you should go to Florida or Texas."

Convincing Ted to plead guilty in Florida to consecutive life sentences and avoiding the death penalty in Florida, Colorado, and Utah (as well as potential charges in Washington) also included imploring by Ted's mother and his new lady friend,

Carole Ann Boone. His public defenders helped a great deal as well, though their involvement was kept from Ted, as he (wrongfully) mistrusted them, as usual. They were dedicated and hardworking people.

After three days of pressuring Ted into accepting the plea agreement, he finally agreed to sign the paperwork and did. Notice was given to the court, the prosecuting attorneys signed the agreement, and a hearing was set for May 31 in Judge Edward Cowart's courtroom. Ted had lucked out again, as Judge Cowart was known as a fine, independent legal mind and not a hack. He was also a very strong believer in the death penalty.

Millard, Ted, and I were exhausted from the marathon discussions we had on the second floor of the Tallahassee jail. Ted's cell had no windows, only light coming from a bulb high on the ceiling, which provided very little illumination. He had a typewriter and a number of boxes full of legal materials, mostly briefs I had sent him on pretrial publicity issues, search and seizure issues, and the constitutionality of the death penalty statutes.

I was looking through one of the files during one of our sessions and noticed that Ted had secreted in a small manila envelope a number of antianxiety pills, which he was supposed to be taking on a daily basis. There were over thirty or forty in the envelope. Alone with Ted during this session, I asked him why he was stockpiling the medication, and he said that if all else failed, he would save the State of Florida money and take his own life. He then laughed.

I did not believe that Ted Bundy would ever take his own life. But there was a side of him that knew he was a bad and evil person, and he probably felt he could take his own life if the "good" side of him prevailed. I knew it never would.

On May 31 we entered the Tallahassee courtroom, where a complete media frenzy ensued outside and inside. We knew this would piss Ted off, as he agreed to the plea only on the condition that it be kept secret until he officially entered into it. He did not want to give the media and the public the satisfaction of seeing him finally say he was *the* Ted. Someone on the prosecutor's side had obviously leaked the news. We walked into the courtroom, Millard in front, followed by Ted and me behind.

As we walked to the defense table, Ted, who looked exhausted and somewhat crazy, turned around to me and said, "I am not going to do it."

I informed Millard, and we took Ted back to the holding cell and had our last conversation as attorneys for Ted Bundy. I will never forget Millard putting his skinny leg up on a chair in the holding cell and very calmly, in his gentlemanly southern drawl, saying, "Ted, John Henry and I have only so much time in this lifetime, and we are going to spend it helping people who actually want to live. Bye." Millard then left Ted and me alone. Ted had ripped up his copies of the plea agreement, but I maintained the originals.

I decided to give up any efforts to assist him as a lawyer. I told him I had been more or less volunteering my time over the past years, attempting to save his life by interceding with his attorneys and providing him legal materials and, on occasion, actual representation.

I thought he did want to die in a dramatic fashion, I said, and was never going to sign a plea agreement. I explained that achieving the plea agreement between multiple states was beyond my imagination, something that took a great deal of effort and would never be an option in the future.

I was extremely disappointed, as I had thought, with the plea deal, my interactions with him would be over that day and he would die decades later in the geriatric ward of the Florida State Penitentiary.

Before I left Ted somewhat graciously explained to me that if he had not gone down the "dark side," he would have wanted to be a defense attorney and help people in trouble with the law. It was very apparent to me that Ted had no understanding of what it meant to be of service to others, except perhaps in an abstract way.

He asked me what I had gotten out of representing him, and I said, "Basically nothing."

I was not angry so much as disheartened, and, frankly, extremely tired. I caught an early morning plane back to Seattle with the expectation that I would not have any further contact with Ted.

Judge Cowart moved the trial to Miami, Florida, and set the beginning date of the trial for June 1979.

Shortly after my return to Seattle I received a letter from Ted dated June 1, the day after I left Tallahassee, though I did not receive it until a few weeks later, probably because of his transfer from Tallahassee to Miami.

The letter was short and to the point, and I believe it was Ted's way of thanking me for my assistance and acknowledging that I was no longer going to be assisting him. It is this side of Ted that charmed many people, because it seemed sincere and from the heart:

Dear John:

During the time you stayed in Tallahassee, we had a chance to discuss at length developments in the case. If you feel anything like I do, you are sick and tired of hearing about the Bundy case.

It was great seeing you and talking with you again. There can be little question as to why you are doing so well in your practice; you are an exceptionally bright and concerned person. You are much more than that, but the way in which you reach out to those whose causes you advocate is extraordinary.

I am fortunate to have had you on my side and there is no adequate manner to express my gratitude for the time and expense you took to come help me, except to give you a deeply felt, quote, "thank you," in every way.

Best regards,

Ted

13

CONFESSIONS

I never thought I would have any face-to-face contact with Ted again, but for his trial, which began on June 25, 1979, I was subpoenaed as both a defense witness and a state's witness to testify about the circumstances surrounding Ted's bizarre phone call to me the night of February 16, 1978.

Ted was acting as his own cocounsel and questioning many of the witnesses during the pretrial hearings as well as during the trial. The defense's theory was that Ted's extremely inculpatory (incriminating) statements were involuntary, because his state of mind was psychotic, and thus none of them should be utilized at the trial.

I testified in detail about my recollection and drew from the notes I took during my conversations with Ted when he was still unknown to his jailers in Florida.

There was little hope, in my opinion, that any judge presiding over the Ted Bundy case would suppress any evidence, much less statements he allegedly made to the police, on tape and off, indicating his guilt in the crimes.

I underestimated the courage and intelligence of Judge Cowart. After my testimony and the testimony of others concerning Ted's state of mind on February 16, Judge Cowart suppressed any and all evidence regarding statements made on tape or otherwise.

Furthermore, he surprised everyone by suppressing all evidence concerning Ted's arrest in Utah and the items found in his car. Both of these rulings were a substantial blow to the prosecution, as they could no longer use Ted's supposed confessions or point out similarities between the stocking mask found in Utah and a stocking mask found at a crime scene in Tallahassee.

I believe that Judge Cowart made these rulings based on his firm belief that they were the correct ones. However, some have speculated that Judge Cowart, as an experienced judge, suppressed the evidence because he knew the state didn't really need it and that Ted Bundy could be convicted without such evidence, thereby limiting potential appeal issues. I come down on the side of Judge Cowart and believe he made these difficult decisions based on his impression of the facts and the law. He was a very fine judge.

I was staying at a Holiday Inn across from the civic center where the trial took place, and Ted was housed in a somewhat new cell in the Dade County jail. The day before my testimony I found him surrounded by guards who were watching him twenty-four hours a day, every second.

I had not seen Ted since his refusal to enter the plea in Tallahassee and wanted to explain to him the purpose of my testimony and get his permission for testifying, as it could involve a violation of the attorney-client privilege. A client can give details of horrific crimes, even murder, and the lawyer can never reveal that information without the client's agreement or a court order. Here my testimony could do nothing to hurt Ted's case, as he made no admissions in the February 16 phone call, just a lot of real crazy comments.

Ted was sprawled on the floor of his cell, and there were tears in his eyes. He had been emotionally upset all day, he said. I sat on the bunk. He stayed on the floor. He looked up and said, "John, I want to be a good person. I am just not."

This was an extraordinary statement, as sociopaths never acknowledge that they are bad individuals. So here I was faced with the most infamous mass murderer in the history of the United States who had been, in my opinion, rightfully diagnosed as a sociopath and who was telling me, in an emotional state, that he knew he was a bad person.

This statement broadened my understanding of why Ted did so many self-destructive things, from becoming easily apprehended after his first escape and taste of freedom to leaving Ann Arbor and Chicago, places easy to recede into, and going to Florida, the center of the Death Belt.

It also would explain how easily he was apprehended in Lake City by an overweight police officer who at the time was chasing someone he had no idea had done anything wrong but was just acting suspicious. This would also explain, perhaps, why Ted actually wanted to die.

I was stunned by his statement. I took a deep breath and told myself to just listen. Still on the floor, he began to describe his first involvement in criminal activity as a young teenager in Tacoma, Washington. He admitted that he was obsessed with "control."

He said he liked to control people even in the most mundane or informal settings, such as gym class and extracurricular activities in junior high and high school. He said that he would go to the local pet store and buy five to ten mice and take them into the woods in a cardboard box. He'd stare into the box and hold a hand over each one, deciding if that particular mouse would go free or die. If the mouse was lucky, he would reach in, rescue it from its cardboard prison, and set it loose in the forest. He would pick the unlucky mice up by the tails, grip their bodies with his other hand, and pull the tails and bodies apart as hard as he could, ripping out their spines, then dispose of the bodies with a toss into the bushes.

He said it was the same with the women he stalked. He would watch them and determine whether he would go further, basically on a whim. There were many times he chose a victim, stalked her for hours, and then determined that he would not assault or kidnap her. This, to him, was a form of "playing God," and he would feel good about exercising his "mercy" when he didn't follow through with his violent impulse.

He said he knew early on that he was wrong to behave this way, but he couldn't control himself. And the more he was able to successfully control other individuals, the more he craved it.

After listening to Ted for half an hour or so, I began to ask him questions and take notes. I asked him whether there was a sexual component to his criminal behavior, and he said there was not. He did admit that he had "sexual relations" with his victims before and after their deaths, but often it was an afterthought. He also sometimes tried to confuse authorities into believing there was more than one perpetrator. In other words, some of the victims would show signs of sexual abuse, and others would not.

He told me that the excitement of stalking and controlling others, and ultimately making the decision as to whether they would live or die, did excite him sexually, which disgusted me thoroughly and made me question, once again, why I was doing anything to help this miserable human being.

I remember long pauses when I would stand up and hold the bars, as if looking for balance, some kind of guidance as to whether I should stay or not. I also vividly remember thinking that I *had* to get out of this business; I just couldn't take it anymore. But I pulled myself together and stayed.

He told me again that when he was a teenager in Tacoma, he killed a fellow teenager, a male. I did not ask any further questions, nor did he provide details except that the victim was approximately his age and the incident started as a sexual exploration game and turned deadly.

It was my impression from Ted's personality and the police reports and psychological evaluations I had read that he committed most of his criminal acts under the influence of at least some alcohol. I asked him the role alcohol played in these offenses, and he admitted that he drank on every occasion, not to the extent of being drunk but to the extent that his compulsions became stronger and his ability to control his behavior was weakened by the alcohol.

It was apparent to me that his use of alcohol triggered the lessening of his humanity, if he had any at all, and was part of his ritual involving the control and the ultimate taking of other people's lives.

He explained he got little satisfaction after the deaths. Once his "prey" was dead the craving began again. He would often revisit the murder sites to have sexual contact with the victims' corpses before moving them, in an effort to gain enough satisfaction to prevent him from killing again soon. At this point I asked to be excused for a break, went to the men's room, and got sick to my stomach. I tried to call my friend and investigator Sylvia Mathews for some advice and solace but was unable to contact her. I returned to the cell.

Ted said that he was not certain of the exact number of individuals he had killed, but it was over one hundred. He told me that he took people's lives in almost every western state as well as in the Northeast, Florida, and some midwestern states.

I asked him whether he had killed anyone between the time of his second escape and the murders in Tallahassee, and he told me he did not but came close in Ann Arbor, stalking a woman and then determining that she was one of the fortunate ones he would allow to live.

He continued. He said that his involvement with me for such a long period of time was because he could never control me, as my participation in his defenses was entirely voluntary. He told me that one of the reasons he originally sought me out as his lawyer was because we were "so much alike."

And Ted revealed this: he had known all along that I had lost a girlfriend and that she had been murdered; though, to my relief, he didn't seem to know any details about Deborah Beeler or her death.

My head was spinning.

I believe Ted was distraught that afternoon and evening before I got there because he was learning he was losing any ability to control the outcome of his case and life. I also believe the small "good" side of Ted had shown up, which explains his opening remark to me about his desire to be a good person.

It was apparent during the lengthy discussion of his criminal behavior that he knew he was evil and more or less had to be stopped.

I asked him specifically about his apprehension in Lake City after the killing of Kimberly Leach and how I thought it seemed almost intentional, as he could have easily outrun an overweight law enforcement officer. He indicated that that was true. He had been intoxicated during the events with Kimberly Leach, and as the alcohol wore off, it became apparent to him that he was completely out of control. The killing of a very young girl was a new direction he was taking, and he was thoroughly disgusted with himself. I know he told the cops that they would not want to find the site of Kimberly Leach's body, as the scene was so disgusting that no human being should be subjected to that vision. (She was found in a pigsty, half eaten by hogs.)

At this point I asked him why he was telling me all this information, as he had never revealed so much to anyone. This question seemed to shock him, as if he had not realized what had transpired between us. A change came over him; he pulled himself together, and he became the usual distant, self-absorbed Ted. He never answered my question.

We eventually got to talking about the pretrial motions set for the next few days—he gave me his permission to testify about our conversations on February 16—and he washed his face in the combination sink and toilet and sat down on the bunk. All the time we were under the constant surveillance of many jail guards who were giving us privacy enough to speak confidentially but obviously watching our every move.

At one point during Ted's emotional breakdown, one of the guards approached me and asked me if Ted needed to see the psychiatrist or a chaplain, and Ted looked up and said, "No thank you."

I asked Ted, in light of all he had just told me, if he wanted me to talk to his attorneys about the possibility of negotiating some kind of plea to avoid the death penalty, and he told me in no uncertain terms not to pursue that option. I knew, given that he had turned down the deal in Tallahassee, that the state would never open the negotiations again, but I thought I would ask him anyway, knowing his answer would be no.

The next day I testified in the motion to suppress Ted's statements. There was further testimony from other individuals who received phone calls from Ted on the sixteenth and had interactions with him on the sixteenth and the seventeenth. The police officers testified about their interactions with him and their opinions that his statements were voluntary and knowing, despite Ted being tired and emotionally distraught.

There was further testimony from Utah police officers about Ted's apprehension in the Volkswagen containing the burglary tools and handcuffs. Ted questioned these cops himself, and did a very poor job. It was obvious the police officers were uncomfortable being questioned by him, but they consistently stated that he voluntarily gave them permission to search his car, and disputed his assertions otherwise.

It was an extremely bizarre scene: Ted Bundy, the mass murderer, was questioning police authorities as his own attorney. Shortly after these hearings Judge Cowart made his stunning ruling suppressing all of the statements and all of the evidence from Utah. It was the last time I saw Ted Bundy in person.

He was later convicted by the jury in Miami. At the time of his sentencing, Judge Cowart remarked that it was a shame that Ted had wasted his life, that he obviously had the capability to lead a productive life and contribute to society. These comments from Judge Cowart were sincere and reported widely, as was his last comment to Ted in his wonderful, grandfatherly southern drawl, "Take care of yourself, son." And with that he sentenced Ted to die in an electric chair.

14

SUCCESS

My involvement in the Ted Bundy case made me a local celebrity. And cases poured in, enough that by the end of the 1970s I was able to buy a big house on the shore of Puget Sound.

As I became better known, rumors about me began to circulate—some of them contradictory. There were rumors that I was a womanizer. Untrue. Though I consider myself a serial monogamist, I have always respected women and have never taken advantage of them. The other gossip was that I was gay.

That particular rumor never bothered me, but I found it puzzling. I have no idea why it came about, maybe because I have female energy and love it. I also enjoy decorating and wearing nice clothes, so perhaps to the simpleminded I *must* be gay.

Stephen Trisko and William Gruver weren't gay either. But that didn't stop them from entering The Monastery, a gay bar in downtown Seattle, on June 30 and July 14, 1979. The men paid the seven-dollar cover charge, ordered drinks, and danced together as if they were lovers.

Then they charged my client, George Freeman, who ran The Monastery, with a liquor violation. Trisko and Gruver were undercover state liquor-enforcement agents. Their case against Freeman, I believed, was based more on antigay discrimination than on liquor laws.

I tested this hypothesis in court. Before the judge, I asked either Trisko or Gruver—I can't remember which—if he and his partner had "held hands." The agent got defensive and flustered but admitted that, yes, as part of their cover, they had held hands. I then asked if he knew *why* he had been chosen for this particular undercover investigation. He again got flustered, looking around the courtroom, worried, I'm sure, that someone might think he seemed gay.

I'd be lying now if I said I didn't take some pleasure in watching the homophobic officer squirm in the witness chair.

Also around this time, I had a strange encounter with my past life in rock and roll. I had a client, Dolores, whom I represented on something small—I can't remember what—in federal court. After I represented her and told her what she owed me, she said, "Oh don't worry. My Uncle Al will pay the bill." She said I'd have to go to his house and retrieve the money. She gave me an address in a poor neighborhood south of the city. So one afternoon I knocked off work early and drove past dilapidated houses until I spotted a beautiful modern home at the address Dolores had given me.

I knocked on the door, and this small black man opened it. He was drunk. I mean, just plastered. He said, "Hi! I'm Al!" Behind him on the wall were Jimi Hendrix's gold records.

I couldn't believe it. "You're Jimi Hendrix's dad, Al!"

"Yeah."

He invited me in and spent the next couple hours getting me drunk. As the afternoon wore on, I told him the story of when I hung out with his son in Denver. When I mentioned the conch belt Jimi had bought, Al stopped me.

"Hang on." He disappeared into a room heaping with memorabilia and emerged with the conch belt raised over his head triumphantly.

We laughed and drank some more.

One of my higher-profile clients during that same era was Duke Fergerson. A wide receiver with the Seattle Seahawks, Duke had been charged with the August 25, 1979, rape of a twenty-two-year-old woman and the rape of a twenty-six-year-old woman on September 10 of the same year. The attacks occurred at expensive condos and apartment units in the Bellevue suburb of Seattle. The only description of the attacker was "good-looking, twenty- to thirty-year-old black male, tall, with short, well-groomed hair." The victims were white. The Bellevue Police Department staked out condo and apartment complexes. Looking for a suspect couldn't be hard, since almost no black people lived in the area. One night they saw a tall, attractive black man pull into the parking lot of a luxury condo in a new BMW. He disappeared into the complex, and the police got the license plate number. (My investigators later learned that a fellow Seahawk lived in the complex and Duke was visiting him after a night on the town.)

The police ran the plate, and it came back to Duke, who lived with his wife in an affluent neighborhood near Bellevue. They pulled up his driver's license photo. Duke was indeed a tall, good-looking black male with short hair. They put together a photo lineup that included Duke, in his Seahawks uniform, and five street junkies with ratty hair and scrubby beards. As I said at the trial, you might as well have had five chickens and a nun in the photo array. The victims made tentative IDs of Duke, the only good-looking black man in the lineup. The cops set up an in-person lineup, and Duke went willingly, without a lawyer, as he knew he had done nothing wrong. Once again, in the live lineup, he stood out. All the others came from the jail, looking down and out. Big surprise: the two victims said that Duke "looked familiar and could be the attacker."

Of course he looked familiar: they had seen his photo the day before, and he was stand-out attractive. The police detectives and two prosecutors (all white) involved in the case charged Duke with two counts of first-degree rape. They leaked the charges to the press and made a high-profile arrest, with TV cameras and newspaper photographers present, at Duke's home as he was pulling into the driveway with his wife. After his arrest he bailed out and hired me.

There was no evidence in the two cases other than the witness identifications and a smudge mark on a wall at one apartment that was similar in color to one of Duke's shoes. I proved at trial that the police detective changed the color of the shoes in his report to match the wall mark (he never seized the shoes). So there was nothing other than the identifications: no DNA, no hair, no fingerprints. Oh, there *were* fingerprints, but they were not Duke's. It was critical to get separate trials, a "severance" in legal terms, which is usually difficult. Prosecutors often stack cases together when they have little evidence, but judges usually don't sever, as it is costly to the courts. After a hard-fought pretrial motion, the judge did separate the trials, which was a decision critical to the outcome.

The all-white prosecution team went after Duke with a vengeance. The cops were intimidated by Duke—his success, his star status, his intelligence, and his good looks. The fact that he had many beautiful, young white women as friends also pissed them off. The prosecutors thought they *had* to have a conviction. They made a big splash in the press when he was charged. For them the case was going to be a career builder or buster.

They were worried because of the poor investigation by the police and the circumstantial nature of the case. I was worried because it was a rape charge against a black man, with white victims, and likely an all-white jury. I was right to worry. Duke was the only black person in the courtroom involved in the trail. No black jurors were in the panel, and the judge was white. There was only one black judge (out of thirty) in King County at the time.

The first case went to trial, and the victim (I say "victim" rather than "alleged victim" as she *was* raped, just not by Duke) was very compelling: young, attractive, less than worldly, from a small town in eastern Washington. She was a racist but didn't know it. The proof of this came during my questioning her on cross-examination. I asked her if the perpetrator had any unusual accent or speech pattern, and she said, "Yes, he did not sound like a black man; he sounded educated!" No shit, that's what she said. The courtroom erupted in sighs and moans. The prosecutors almost fell out of their chairs. Her answer won the case for me. She had no black friends, had known no black people in her past, and picked Duke out of the lineup because he was the only man who fit the description of the rapist.

After losing, the prosecutors licked their wounds and proceeded with the second case. It was just as weak as the first, but they were desperate to save face and tried hard to get a conviction. The jury was split eleven to one for acquittal; the hold-out juror said the fact that the rapist had a mustache and Duke never did was immaterial since "you can't see a moustache on a black man." The ordeal cost him a lot of worry and money, but Duke was a free man.

After his football career was over he became successful in business and an advocate for early learning reading projects. I once saw him on Sesame Street supporting literacy.

My career was also flying high. I had four cars, a motorcycle, a waterfront house, two Rolexes, and a Ralph Lauren model as a girlfriend. But I'd be lying if I said my life was in order.

Remember back in 1970 when Jasper, the inmate at the DC jail, told me to never try cocaine because I'd like it too much?

Yeah, well I should have listened to him. I got around to trying it, and he was right. My friends and I partied hard, though never when there was a trial.

I'd frequently buy a bottle of cognac just to calm my nerves from all the coke I was doing. There's a photo of me from that era. I'm sitting on my couch in a bathrobe, and I look emaciated. Seriously, just skin and bones.

15

"THE FLOOR IS SUPPOSED TO BE GREEN"

The sky had just begun to pale on a February morning when I stepped out of the house of a friend and fellow lawyer in the Leschi neighborhood, just a few blocks from the shores of Lake Washington. The tree branches overhead looked like arteries running through the sky. My head still rang with cocaine, and my tongue, dehydrated from sipping cognac all night, felt like a slab of pumice in my mouth. Another all-nighter. At least it was Saturday.

I folded myself into my black Mercedes and cut over to Yesler Avenue, bound for State Route 509 and, ultimately, my waterfront house fifteen miles away in Normandy Park, where coffee and a hot shower awaited. Along the way I slid past the

King County courthouse and the police station, and, shit . . . there were a dozen police cruisers, marked and unmarked, and other emergency vehicles pulling in and out. Something big had happened. I was in no condition to stop and talk to a bunch of cops to find out what it was. A car full of homicide detectives, all of whom I knew, passed me. Sgt. Joe Sanford looked me right in the eye and nodded. I responded with a blank, dazed stare. They wheeled toward Chinatown, and I steered in the opposite direction, toward 509 and home.

I cleaned up, brewed a pot of coffee, and around 7:00 AM turned on the television. All the local stations were broadcasting live from the mouth of a dank, garbage-strewn alley off King Street (around the corner from the popular Asian food joints I frequented). The news anchors were unusually grim and obviously moved by the events they were reporting. I could see medical examiner trucks and men carrying what were unmistakably body bags through the alley. There was no end to the parade of bags, it seemed. Donald Reay, Seattle's internationally known coroner, and his staff streamed in and out of a four-story brick building.

Slowly I pieced together the story flashing on the screen. Earlier that morning, February 19, 1983, a little after midnight, fourteen Chinese residents of Seattle, many well known and influential, were found shot in the Wah Mee Club, a not-so-secret underground gambling establishment. Most had been hog-tied and shot in the back of the head. There was one survivor, an eyewitness. Thirteen dead. The reporters were calling it the largest-ever mass murder on the West Coast.

I stayed rapt in front of the screen for hours until, around noon, I received a phone call from my answering service. On the line was Steven Ng, whose brother Benjamin I'd previously represented in juvenile court in a minor theft case. Steven told me Ben had been arrested for the murders, and asked if I'd go see his little brother at the police station immediately.

Benjamin was twenty years old, short and slight, with almost feminine good looks and the perpetual appearance of a trapped kitten about to be eaten by a pit bull. He and his family had emigrated from Hong Kong in 1975. (His parents had escaped to Hong Kong from the Guangdong Province in mainland China by swimming the Yangtze River.) They were well educated in Asia but held menial jobs in America: his father was a cook; his mother labored in a garment factory. His four older siblings were hard workers too. Only Ben lived outside the law, and had since his early teens: he had been picked up for the strong-arm robbery of an eleven-year-old at age fifteen, shoplifting at seventeen, and shooting at four men after a fight at eighteen (charges were dropped after investigators discovered he had acted in self-defense). He craved the affluence of the people he saw on American television, drove a blue 1977 Corvette, and wore a Rolex watch and designer clothes. His family clearly loved and adored him but were embarrassed by his excesses. When I first represented him as a young teen I got special permission from the juvenile jail for his mother and father to enter his cell so they could rub Chinese herbs on his chest for a slight cold. Even then he seemed to order his parents around. And they seemed to fear him, like if they didn't do as asked, he would explode.

My hangover fading, I drove back to the city, where I had no trouble getting through the intense security at the King County jail at the top of the courthouse. The entire homicide division was there. I doubt they were happy to see me. They rarely were. They knew I'd do my job and get Ben to shut up. I was escorted to the smallest holding cell. Ben was alone with a blanket around him and nothing on but boxer shorts. His clothing and shoes had been taken as evidence. His long black hair stuck out all over like one of those wild-haired troll dolls. He had that trapped cat look on his face but hardly seemed aware of the gravity of the situation. The first words out of his mouth were "How long until I get released?"

He was, until I told him, unaware that an eyewitness had survived and identified him and his friend Kwan Fai "Willie" Mak as the killers. Wai Chin, the frail survivor, had said there was a third perpetrator, whose identity was still unknown. Willie Mak was also in custody, but Ben didn't know that either until I informed him. The one thing I didn't have to tell Ben was to shut up. He hadn't said a word to the cops.

I knew nothing of the facts of the case, just the horror. And Ben wasn't forthcoming with information, which was fine, as I knew if I took the case, the details would come later. I spent about an hour with him before we ran out of things to talk about.

I met with his family next. I knew it would be a death penalty case and expensive to defend. They said they only had $25,000 to pay me. At the time defending a capital case usually cost at least a million dollars, with the results often being the imposition of the ultimate penalty. A certainty was that thirteen well-loved and respected individuals had been gunned down like cattle in a slaughterhouse.

I told the family I'd need some time to decide.

The Wah Mee Club had operated, off and on, as a gambling den and speakeasy since the 1920s and had recently been leased to the Suey Sing Association, rumored to be a Chinese *tong*, a type of community organization sometimes thought to be a criminal enterprise. The illegal gambling, more or less tolerated by the police, ran from midnight, when the surrounding restaurants closed, until dawn. The most popular game was pai gow, played with Chinese dominoes. Some of the International District's wealthiest and most politically connected individuals attended nightly, as did numerous restaurant employees just off their shifts. Backed by powerful Chinese businessmen who had ponied up $10,000 to $20,000 each to bankroll the operation, the gambling was high stakes—up to $1,000 a bet. It wasn't uncommon for there to be at least tens of thousands of dollars on hand. Security was tight. The fear was not just of potential robbery but also of rival tongs making power plays. Patrons had to pass through three steel doors and the scrutiny of at least two security guards. The first door, tucked into a green-walled entryway off the alley, had to be buzzed open, with access granted only to those whom the guards could identify through a clear glass brick that functioned as a peephole. Patrons were then allowed through a second door and into a small anteroom, searched, and buzzed into the lounge and main gaming area, a sixty-by-one-hundred-foot space with four felt-top gambling tables.

Willie Mak and Ben Ng were known at the club. Willie was a gambler, and police believed he owed gambling debts of more than $100,000 and had hatched a plan to rob and kill those in the club, enlisting Ben Ng and another friend, Tony Ng (no relation to Ben), as accomplices. Ben was known to be volatile and easily incited to commit crimes, especially when prompted by Willie. Tony was unknown to the club members.

Detectives believed the three men entered a little before midnight, easily gaining access because the guards recognized Ben and Willie. Once inside they drew their weapons—likely .22- or .25-caliber handguns—and ordered the nine or ten people already inside to lie on the floor. They removed the victims' money and wallets and bound their hands and feet with white nylon rope. As more people arrived, the trio ordered the newcomers to the floor and tied them up. Once they had a total of fourteen hostages—thirteen men and one woman, mostly in their fifties or early sixties—the gunmen opened fire, shooting them at point-blank range in the head.

They fled with about $20,000, not knowing Wai Chin was still alive. The sixty-one-year-old wrested free of the ropes and stumbled into the alley, where incoming patrons were able to help him. Right away he identified Willie Mak and Ben Ng as two of the three perpetrators. Ben and Willie were arrested within hours at their south Seattle homes. (Ben was living with his girlfriend at her parents' house.) In an affidavit prosecutor William Downing stated that, along with a total of ten firearms, police recovered more than $10,000 cash in Ben's bedroom, where he was sleeping with his girlfriend, and more than $5,000 in Willie's bedroom.

I knew if I took the case, I'd be in for the biggest fight of my career. I also knew I'd probably go broke. I was tired of evil in my life. I was tired of taking cases for a lot less money than they would cost. I also knew, because it seemed like such an open-and-shut case, that no one needed a defense against the death penalty more than Benjamin Ng. If there was ever justification for capital punishment, Ben's actions qualified. I'd do everything I could to save his life, and still probably lose. But I had to try.

I phoned his family and told them I was in.

A day or two after the killings I visited the crime scene along with Sgt. Joe Sanford and another cop, guys I respected immensely. They hadn't muscled into Ben's cell to pressure him as bad cops often do. They had honored his invocation of his right to remain silent. Sanford had even told me before I entered the jail that Ben had invoked and they'd questioned him no further—just one example of how different the Seattle Homicide Unit was compared to other police agencies. Here they were faced with the most horrible case they'd ever encountered and needed to do all they could to allay community fear and solve the case, but they had backed off as true professionals when Ben invoked his rights. This division, led by Sanford and another sergeant, Don Cameron, was the absolute best in the country. Unsurpassed by younger cops, these were old-school, cigar-smoking, hard-drinking detectives who worked long hours and set an ethical standard. A little rough around the edges, they swore often, let their shirttails hang out, and ate food on the run. They did not look like Tom Selleck or Don Johnson, but they were the best. At that point I'd handled at least twenty murder cases investigated by their division and was allowed free reign of the fifth-floor offices that always had half-eaten sandwiches, strong coffee, and cigarette smoke. I was honored on at least three occasions when they sent clients my way. They weren't supposed to make such referrals but did so if they thought a person needed an aggressive attorney, usually self-defense cases where they had to make an arrest but felt the defendant was probably justified in using deadly force.

As we entered the alley, past an Indonesian-American-owned aquarium and bird shop, a decorative kite the shape of a goldfish wagging in the wind overhead, Joe warned me that the sight inside Wah Mee was hard to stomach. Dried blood speckled the pavement in front of the club door, likely left by survivor Wai Chin when he staggered out of the gambling den for help.

We paused in front of the entrance, lit cigars, and spread Vick's Vapor Rub on our upper lips to mask the stench that was about to assault us. We crept through the club's multiple doors, down a short, dimly lit hallway, and into the main gallery. We stepped along a path of newspapers laid out on the ground toward a set of folding chairs, and sat. The club looked much smaller than I'd expected. An elegantly curved cocktail bar split the room, with an upper-level lounge on one side and the gaming area on the other, lower level. Lamps, tasseled and spherical, hung from the low ceiling. A large gong stood in the corner. Ornate Oriental columns were spaced out every few feet, black at the bases, their tops red, nearly matching the color of the floor. It was eerily quiet, with only the buzz of flies to break the silence. I stared at the dark crimson floor, collecting my thoughts, not knowing what to say.

"John!" Joe's gruff voice called out as if half a mile away. "The floor. It's supposed to be green. Green, John—not red!"

I sat up and took in the scene again. Blood from at least fourteen head wounds had painted the club's emerald floor a horrific scarlet. I thought of the victims, tied up and awaiting their turns when their skulls would meet the muzzle of the assailants' guns, of the fear they must have felt in this casino-turned-abattoir. My stomach turned, and once again that *What am I doing with my life?* feeling seized my guts. I gnawed at my cigar, jotted as many observations as I could, and left.

At home in Normandy Park I made a vow. As with every case, no drugs or alcohol. Not when preparing for the case. Not during the pretrial. And not during the trial. Defending Benjamin Ng would be the greatest challenge of my professional life, and I needed a clear head.

Next I called my dad. I told him what little I could about the case, the gruesome details already made public, and he listened. When I finished he fell silent for a few seconds. "Somebody has to do your job," he said evenly. "I'm just sad it has to be you."

16

DEFENDING BENJAMIN NG

On Tuesday, February 22, 1983, three days after the massacre, I stood with Benjamin Ng in front of Judge Betty Taylor Howard for a bail hearing. Ben wore a gray prison jumper and his head was again a riot of long black hair, a combination that made him look smaller than ever. To our left stood Willie Mak, in a red jumper, and his attorney, John Wolfe. The four of us, along with the judge and six armed guards, stood in a fishbowl of bulletproof glass, separating us from the gallery crammed with Ben's still-stunned family and about two dozen members of the media. The third suspect, Tony Ng, as yet unknown to reporters, was still at large, bolstering the prosecutors' argument that Willie and Ben should not be released on bail. The judge agreed. Ben and Willie were carted off to their cells.

Willie's attorney and I were friendly casual acquaintances, but we clashed on this case from the start. He emphasized the importance of the mitigation package, which would be our attempt to convince the prosecutors to not seek the death penalty. A useless task, I thought. Our clients were charged with thirteen counts of aggravated first-degree murder. There would be no mitigating factors that could lead to avoiding death penalty charges. More important, I knew the process would alert the prosecution to our possible defense strategies.

Wolfe vehemently disagreed. Because this would be such a high-profile case, he said, we had to do everything right or we'd be publically criticized by death penalty experts—likely jealous they didn't get the case—who'd be second-guessing our every move. "That's a bullshit motive," I said, "a cover-your-ass approach." Wolfe later added that we should do everything to appear like we knew what we were doing, appearances being more important than substance. That pissed me off. "OK, that can be *your* goal," I told him, "but it will *never* be my goal!" My goal—my job!—was to save the life of Benjamin Ng.

On Friday, three days after the bail hearing, we stood with our clients on the tenth floor of the King County courthouse in front of another judge for the formal arraignment. He asked that the names of the deceased be read aloud. The bailiff called out all thirteen—"Chong Chin, Henning Chinn, Hung Fat Gee"—and noted that each name—"Chinn Lee Law, John Loui, Dewey Mar, George Mar, Jack Mar"—represented one count of aggravated first-degree murder—"Moo Minn Mar, Wing Chin, Wing Wong."

Ben and Willie pled not guilty. After the guards escorted them away, Wolfe and I stepped out of the courtroom and into a throng of reporters in the hallway. One thing on which Wolfe and I agreed was that we were already, at this early stage, losing the media battle. Two days earlier, on February 23, 1983, the *Seattle Times* ran a profile of Ben (SUSPECT HAS HISTORY OF TROUBLE) that referred to him as a "black sheep," detailed his past crimes, and suggested he was a member of the Hop Sing Tong, a rival of the tong that leased the Wah Mee. Wolfe, meanwhile, was fighting to keep a section of a search warrant affidavit redacted, five lines that revealed that Mak had told a detective shortly after his arrest, "I shot them all." Although no one in the media knew the content of these lines, both the *Times* and the *Seattle Post-Intelligencer* had hired lawyers to unredact them. The information would severely damage Mak's defense.

"The media have reacted hysterically," I admonished the reporters outside the courtroom. I think Wolfe appreciated that.

The King County prosecutor, Norm Maleng, a man I respected greatly even though we were sworn adversaries, had of course assigned his A Team to the case: deputy prosecutors Robert Lasnik and William Downing, both very smart and experienced. I had tried many cases with them—winning some, losing some. Low-key, with great senses of humor, they were difficult opponents. Unlike many prosecutors I could count on, they didn't get distracted by silly issues. They concentrated on the real tasks. Juries and judges liked and respected them. So did I.

They proved as sharp as I'd feared during the next step, the critical assignment of a trial judge. King County at the time had many gifted, experienced, no-nonsense judges—my favorite. There were also a few loose canons who were just plain evil, dumb, or both. We asked for preassignment of a judge and were given a list of three. The prosecutors could strike one, Wolfe and I could strike another, and the third would be assigned the case. The three we had to pick from were all known as anti-defense and pro-prosecution. Not a good omen. We ended up with Judge Frank Howard, a very conservative judge and a very conservative person in general. He was smart but seemed to have no lighter side and was in constant fear that I would take over his courtroom, as was my reputation with less secure judges.

This played out early on when, in mid-March, Lasnik and Downing insisted survivor Wai Chin have his testimony videotaped. Lasnik told Judge Howard that Wai Chin, the only eyewitness to the massacre, could die before the trial, then scheduled for July 1, a little more than three months away. The prosecutors said they wanted to have Chin's testimony videotaped in advance in case he wasn't around when it came time to testify in front of the jury. Chin, who'd sustained bullet wounds to the neck and jaw (two small bits of lead remained lodged in his neck), had already been released from his month-long convalescence at Harborview Medical Center. But Lasnik pointed to an episode earlier in the month, two weeks after the shooting, when the witness's blood pressure dropped and he required resuscitation. Most sensationally, Lasnik also raised the possibility that Chin could be assassinated before the trial.

"The press is going to have a field day with a statement like that!" I objected. Judge Howard called a recess.

Out in the hallway I heard Lasnik tell a reporter, "They want [Chin] to die." *They* referring to Wolfe and me. I lost my shit. Back in court I told the judge what I'd heard. Lasnik apologized and backed down. He dropped the assassination attempt argument altogether and asked that the record show that his only case for the videotaped testimony was Chin's ailing health. Swayed by the testimony of two doctors who said the witness, a lifelong smoker, was at risk of developing serious pulmonary problems, Judge Howard said he was leaning toward allowing the videotaped testimony.

A *Seattle Times* editorial a few days later, on March 28, 1983, piled on: "The precautions sought by the prosecution, and tentatively approved by the court, in preserving testimony of the sole survivor of the Wah Mee Club massacre are warranted under the circumstances. And it is difficult to see how they could jeopardize the rights of the defendants." The prosecutors were smart. I could see what they were up to, even if the media—and, apparently, Judge Howard—could not. What they really wanted was a dry run of dramatic testimony that would be publicized and further taint the prospective jurors.

I was tired of Lasnik and Downing being one step ahead of me. No more letting them lead this dance. I'd spoken with Chin's doctors, who said he was in good health and his prognosis was good. So, unbeknownst to Judge Howard or the prosecutors, I subpoenaed the doctors to the next hearing, which was well attended by the media, with standing room only.

The courtroom blew up. The prosecutors and the judge accused me of all types of misconduct. "If the issue is his health, here are his doctors," I said. "What's the big deal?"

Judge Howard turned bright red. "From now on," he yelled, "you need permission to issue subpoenas."

I walked up forcefully to his bench and pointed my finger at him. "I will never follow that order!" It was my client's right to call witnesses and issue subpoenas. He might as well find me in contempt now, I said. I held out my hands for the jailers to cuff me.

That shocked the judge. He called a recess. Lasnik and Downing wouldn't look at me. Wolfe either. Still, when he came back half an hour later, Judge Howard recanted his order barring me from issuing subpoenas without permission. I respected him for that. He remained irritated with me, but he seemed to understand I was doing my job and doing it well. After all, no one ever entertained the notion that Ben would not, ultimately, get the death penalty.

Meanwhile, my annoyance with Wolfe bloomed. He sat on his hands during the whole scuffle over the doctors. And we lost: Howard ultimately allowed Chin's testimony to be videotaped.

On Tuesday, May 10, Wolfe, our clients, and I, along with Lasnik and Downing, reported to Judge Howard's courtroom at 1:30 PM. The gallery was empty—no media, no families, just a handful of armed guards, a court reporter, and a video technician. Wai Chin sat in the witness chair, the camera lens trained on him and a whiteboard with the layout of the Wah Mee Club superimposed on it.

Downing examined the witness first:

"Would some of the people that came [to the Wah Mee Club] have a lot of money?"

Chin: "Some of them."

"I object," I said. "The question is leading."

Downing tried again: "What sort of people came to the club?"

Chin detailed the club's clientele, its hours, and its layout, before the questions delved into when my client arrived on the night of the shooting.

Downing: "And it was soon after 12:00 when Mr. Ng arrived?"

"Objection," I said. "Leading."

When the prosecutor asked Chin what happened after he left the club and stumbled, wounded, into the alley, where he found people to help him, the witness answered, "Then I tell them we had been robbed here. They asked me who, black guy or what else, Vietnam guy, and I said, 'No, Ng and Mak.'"

"I object," I said. "Object to the hearsay from the other parties."

It went on like this, as is expected between the defense and prosecution. It's when Wolfe examined the witness that things got awkward. He pushed against the prosecutor's contention that his client was the ringleader. Fair enough. That's his job. But his questions began to imply that *my* client was the ringleader.

Referring to a witness statement Chin signed weeks earlier, Wolfe said, "And the only reference in that paragraph to Mr. Mak is that he pulled a gun out after Mr. Ng came and that he helped the third man put the wallets in a brown bag; isn't that true?"

I'd had enough. I opposed Wolfe in front of our shared adversaries. When he made a reference to Tony Ng, a suspect still at large, I intoned, "I object. Nobody has been identified as Tony Ng."

It became increasingly apparent to me that if Ben had any chance of making it out of this thing alive, he'd have to be tried separately from his friend. There was much more damaging evidence against Willie: it was his idea and his motive—he needed the money to pay gambling debts. He also had bad energy that would affect the trial. With separate trials, I'd be able to do everything possible to blame Willie and cast Ben as a tool Willie had used.

But I didn't throw Wolfe and Mak under the bus just then. When my turn to examine Chin came around, I tried something different.

Me: "Mr. Chin, who shot you?"

Chin: "I don't know."

"Mr. Chin, who shot John Loui?"

"I don't know either."

"Who shot Wing Wong?"

I knew, based on previous statements, that Chin, tied up and on his stomach the night of the massacre, had not seen my client shoot anyone. I also knew that police had only recovered bullets from two guns. Two guns, three shooters? There was room for doubt.

I continued: "Who shot Wing Wong?"

"I don't know. I don't know nothing."

"Who shot C. Chong?"

"Don't know."

We went through every name. It would be a strategy I'd use if I secured separate trials for Ben and Willie. With Chin unable to say who shot whom, I could plant a seed of uncertainty in the jury: maybe someone else—Tony or Willie—did the killing. If only I could cut the tether between Ben and Willie.

So I couldn't believe my luck when, on Friday, May 27, seemingly out of nowhere, Wolfe withdrew from the case, citing a conflict of interest (a matter unrelated to the case but that a judge agreed created an ethical dilemma). Two new public defenders were assigned to Mak. The accused were still slated to be tried together, but I was one step closer to my goal.

At a hearing on June 1, I told Judge Howard I wanted the trial to begin August 1, knowing that Mak's new attorneys, Don Madsen and Jim Robinson, would ask for a much later date in order to familiarize themselves with the nearly twelve hundred pieces of discovery dropped on their doorstep after Wolfe bowed out. They requested October 1.

The prosecution knew what I was up to and clearly saw that a separate trial would benefit Ng. They insisted on a trial date of August 22, the last possible date by which Mak and Ng could be tried together, thanks to my earlier invoking of Ben's right to a speedy trial. Arguing against the separate trial, Lasnik pointed to potential security risks, the high cost of two separate trials, and the fact that media coverage of the first trial would prejudice the jury of the second. (*Now* he was concerned about prejudicing the jury!)

Two days later, at another hearing, I reiterated that I refused to waive my client's access to a speedy trial and reminded the court that disregarding Ng's right in this matter could result in the dismissal of all charges against him.

But Downing was quick. He reminded the court that back in May I had said I'd need much more time, until at least August 22. (He was right.) A week later, after further deliberation, Judge Howard gave me the date I now said I wanted—August 1—but still refused to grant separate trials (which is what I was really after).

I felt the judge was calling my bluff.

We did receive one bit of good news around this time: a judge assigned David Wohl to join the Ng defense team at the court's expense. The request had been stalled because the court believed Ben Ng had money, due in part to his sleek blue Corvette. But we were able to demonstrate that Ben was broke—his sister had paid for the car—and the family had no more money for legal fees.

Wohl was a sharp attorney, and I welcomed the help.

Now it was Mak's lawyers' turn to irritate Judge Howard. They said that unless they could be given more time to prepare, they would have to drop out of the case and Mak would need to be assigned yet another defense team. Of course, the judge didn't like threats. On July 15 he denied their request to delay the trial and ordered them not to withdraw as Mak's attorneys.

Finally, on Wednesday, August 3, after an eight-hour hearing during which both defense teams pled the case for separate trials, Judge Howard relented. Jury selection for our trial would begin immediately, and the Mak trial would begin two weeks after the Ng verdict was reached.

It was a welcome triumph. Now I could focus on the task of casting Ben as a follower in the whole murderous enterprise and raise the question of whether he actually shot two of the guns used in the slaying.

There was more: while developing my relationship with Ben I noticed something strange when he answered questions. If I held up a pencil and asked what it was, he would say "Wood." If I showed him a watch, he'd say "Time." Point to a shoe and he would say "Protector of foot," not "Shoe." It wasn't a language barrier; Ben spoke perfect English. I asked his family about head injuries in the past and learned that when Ben was an infant in Hong Kong some apparently crazy lady in the market started yelling to the crowd that Ben was the devil and beat him on the head with a two-by-four. Ben was hospitalized for weeks and, according to his family, was never quite the same. Based on my observations and the family's input, I had Ben tested at Harborview Medical Center for head trauma. The doctors concluded that Ben suffered from dementia due to an injury to the left side of his brain, the area that controls judgment.

We began jury selection on Monday, August 8. The Benjamin Ng who showed up in court that morning would be unrecognizable to anyone who'd seen him during much of the pretrial or in the days leading up to the murders. Gone was his mop. His hair was cut short, with Spock-like square bangs. A classy button-down shirt under a wool vest and pressed slacks gave him the look of a college debate champ, not the street thug the prosecution and the media had tried to paint him as. This was the work of Ben's pretty nineteen-year-old girlfriend, Kennis Izumi, of Chinese descent but born and raised in Seattle. She and my client had dated since high school, and she stuck by him, showing up at court all through the months of pretrial, even camping out in the hall on days she wasn't allowed in the courtroom. Her beauty and her devotion to an accused mass murderer made her a media favorite. Large photos of her appeared next to front-page, top-of-the-fold news articles about the Wah Mee massacre.

That day we started with a pool of about two hundred prospective jurors. By late afternoon we removed all who could not sit because they were against the death penalty (you can't be a juror in a capital case unless you believe in capital punishment), had other hardships, or admitted they just could not be fair. We were left with about a hundred people. The work of finding at least one juror who would hold out for life began. (You only need one vote for a life sentence, as a death verdict must be unanimous.)

This was also a good time to test out a strategy, one I had begun to develop during Wai Chin's videotaped testimony. I asked the members of the remaining jury pool, all believers in the death penalty, if a brain injury would be enough to find Ng not guilty or, if convicted, to spare his life? *No.* Would the fact that he was the tool of Willie Mak be enough? *No.* Would the fact that there might be some tong rivalry going on be enough? *No.* OK, would the fact that three participants only used two guns and the eyewitness could not ID who the shooters were be enough? *Maybe.* So this became my theme: brain injury plus Willie's manipulation plus two guns and three participants and no certainty about who shot and who didn't.

Picking a "death-qualified" jury is an art, not a science. I immediately spotted people my gut told me I did not want on the jury. One fellow, from remote Vashon Island, wore a Jack Daniel's baseball cap and a belt buckle that said WINCHESTER ARMS. He spent the first one or two days listening to the questioning of other jurors about life and death, some real emotional questions and answers. I could tell he paid attention. His number came up, and he was seated in the front row of the jury box. The prosecutors thought they had their boy and asked very few questions. I could tell something was bothering him, so I walked up to him and asked, "What's wrong?" He broke down and said that he had always been a strong believer in the death penalty but after sitting in court listening to the questions and answers, he realized he could never vote to put that young man to death. The good news was all the other jurors heard this heartfelt response; the bad news was we lost him as a juror because he said he would not impose the death penalty.

We completed jury selection after five days and ended up with eight men and four women. They ranged from a brewery worker to a Boeing engineer, a retired University of Washington accountant to an IRS examiner. All of them were pro–death penalty. I had to convince just one to spare Benjamin Ng's life. The trial would begin in the morning, Tuesday, August 16.

The day of reckoning was here. The media had dubbed it the highest-profile trial Seattle had ever seen. A crime scene riddled with intrigue, with secret entrances and a history that dated back to the 1920s. Three young suspects, one (Ben) with a Hollywood actress–type girlfriend. Then there were the inherent, palpable evil of Willie Mak and the relative innocence of still at-large Tony Ng. Add the gifted, upwardly mobile prosecutors (both would go on to become respected judges) and the supposed flamboyance of the defense team (me). There had been daily reports for months over the magnitude and intrigue of the trial.

The talking heads on TV, the Nancy Graces of their day—stupid, simpleminded, and pandering to the lowest common denominator—were second-guessing all the decisions the prosecutors and defense lawyers made. There was considerable talk among self-appointed death penalty experts that I should not be doing the case, as I was not recognized as an expert in the field. They pointed to all the choices I'd made over the previous six months: I hadn't pursued a mitigation package to talk the prosecutors out of the death penalty charge; I forced the case to trial too quickly; I picked a jury in five days, which many experts think is malpractice, as most death penalty jury selections take months, using expensive jury consultants; I didn't use all my preemptory challenges, waiving many jury issues on appeal, which is a big no-no with the experts; and, finally, I left an IRS agent on the jury. This was all proof, they thought, that I had no idea what I was doing. They predicted Ben would be sentenced to death because of my incompetence.

That morning I wore, as was my custom during trials, a thirteen-dollar Timex watch as a good luck charm, and stood in front of the jury for my opening statement. I spent the next thirty minutes telling them that, yes, Benjamin Ng was at the Wah Mee Club on the morning of February 19, 1983, and, yes, he participated in the robbery. But, I said, my client didn't know the murders would take place and left the scene without a drop of blood on him. "It was undisputed that Mak was the leader," I said.

My investigators, Sylvia Mathews and Chris Beck, found as much dirt as they could on Willie, and I intended to use it, along with expert medical testimony on Ben's brain injury, and of course the matter of two guns, three perpetrators.

In a death penalty case there are two phases. The first is the fact phase: Has the government proven its case (here, thirteen counts of premeditated murder) beyond a reasonable doubt? The second, the penalty phase, asks if there are any mitigating circumstances that warrant a life sentence.

Only one juror need answer yes and you've beaten a death sentence. So you don't want to go through some elaborate song and dance about how your client is innocent if you know they will be convicted in phase one and you need the jury to trust you in phase two. Many lawyers make this mistake. Juries are unforgiving. It cannot be understated how much gaining their trust can control the outcome of a verdict. As a result one of my basic rules is never lie to a jury. Withholding evidence is OK, but never lie or make a promise you can't keep. If you do so even on one small point, you'll lose them.

So during the fact phase I focused mostly on the point that only two of the three perpetrators fired guns and Wai Chin did not know which two. We avoided some wild theories about tong intrigue, coercion, and duress, which came up in Mak's trial two weeks later. Keep in mind we never said Ben was not a shooter, only that the state could not prove he was.

The first phase of the trial lasted just six days, as many of the facts were not disputed. The verdict, on Wednesday, August 24, came quickly: guilty of thirteen counts of first-degree murder. For the penalty phase, which took up all of the following day, we put on evidence about Ben's brain injury and how his judgment was impaired, and did so in a way that observers to this day say changed Seattle judicial history.

King County prosecutor Norm Maleng had assigned his A Team to the case. Now I had mine: Ben's mother spoke no English whatsoever, and all the interpreters had turned us down for fear of retribution in the community. So Judge Howard allowed Ben's older brother, Steven, to interpret for her. People thought I was behind it, but I had nothing to do with what happened next.

His mother, Shun Ling Wong Ng, showed up in traditional Chinese dress: silk everything, traditional cap, and turned up shoes. I had no idea she would appear this way until she entered the courtroom. She told the story of how the crazed woman had assaulted Ben in the marketplace in Hong Kong, hitting him with a board and calling him the devil. Ben was less than two at the time. Mrs. Ng broke down but finished her testimony. Steven then began guiding her past the jury box. She paused, turned to the jury, bowed, put her hands in a prayer position, and said in halting English, "Please don't kill my son. Thank you."

She turned and left. The moment was so powerful, Judge Howard had to take a long recess.

The penalty verdict came back quickly—after just two and a half hours. Not a good sign. We had reason to worry. (Weeks later Willie Mak received the death penalty, though it was reduced to life without parole after years of appeals; Tony Ng received thirty years to life and was deported to Hong Kong after serving twenty-eight years.) But when our verdict was read we had *five* life votes. We only needed one. One of the life voters was the IRS agent I had kept on the jury, a much-criticized decision by the self-appointed death penalty experts.

Saving Benjamin Ng's life was the most dramatic and unexpected victory of my career and remains so. I still occasionally hear from Ben (now serving a life sentence) and his family and always receive a Christmas card with good wishes and thank-yous. The family knows he participated in a horrendous event that changed Seattle forever. But they are grateful he was not murdered by the state.

The day after the verdict I was interviewed live on the local NBC affiliate, and the interviewer seemed greatly pissed that Ben's life was spared. She asked how I could justify such a result. I looked at her with pity and said simply, "There has been enough killing."

17

I WANT A NEW DRUG

I had abstained from drugs and alcohol for the three months prior to and during the trial, so my friends and I started celebrating with coke and alcohol up in my Smith Tower office shortly after the verdict. We ran out of coke at about 2:00 AM. I couldn't reach my dealer on the phone, but I was determined to keep the party going.

I was wearing my most expensive suit, Ralph Lauren, and slipped into the seat of my old but pristine black Mercedes Benz 280SE 4.5, an eye-catcher with personalized license plates—a gift from some cops I'd successfully represented—that said ACQUIT. The whole picture was not subtle.

I drove to a seedy part of town to break into my dealer's apartment. It was raining of course, and I parked my car in the alley. I left it running and jumped on the fender to get over the backyard fence. My pant leg caught on a nail, and I fell into a pool of rainwater and cat shit. I looked up and saw the rain coming over the fence and the lights from my car. I said to myself, *There is something wrong with this picture.* Of course, this event did not deter my obtaining what I wanted from my dealer's apartment, which was open. I sped to the office and continued to party in my now smelly and wet suit. But the irony was not lost on me. I had gone from saving a young man's life and being on national television to lying in a pool of cat crap, all within the space of a few hours.

By this time I was on magazine covers and had been dubbed one of Seattle's most eligible bachelors. (What a joke! I was married to my ego.) I'd developed a national reputation as a very well-respected defense lawyer and was giving speeches and press interviews. But I hated myself. I remember reading a magazine article about myself while very drunk and high. It was the only way I could deal with success.

I couldn't shake the cat shit incident. I knew there was a great big hole in my life I was trying to fill with drugs, alcohol, cars, and women. I was miserable and started to look around for solutions to my self-destruction. The answer came while I was in Death Valley cleaning floors and toilets at a retreat center run by Richard Moss.

My good friend and investigator at the time was a women named Sylvia Mathews. She saw how I was falling apart, and cared. She had decided to go to a ten-day intensive retreat at Richard's ranch in Death Valley and invited me along. We didn't really know what Richard did but had seen major changes in a mutual friend who followed Richard's work. Our friend could not really describe the process of what went on, which should have been my first clue that I was in for a wild ride. I was so unaware of the profound nature of Richard's work that I brought along my tennis racket! By the end of the second day my life had been completely transformed and I had been, not so gently, introduced to the mystery of awareness. As Van Morrison, sage and seeker that he is, said, "Never give a sucker an even break / When he's breaking through to a new level of consciousness / There always seems to be more obstacles in the way."

Richard's work is not therapy or religion. It is about what Joseph Campbell called the feeling of being "radically alive" and developing intimacy with life. Richard once said to me that "the depth of the attention (not intention) we give to this moment is the definition of intimacy." So it's all about living in the present, a concept easy to grasp but almost impossible to live. I once said, in a prayer in a sweat lodge, "God grant me the wisdom to live from (not for) this moment and the courage to do it over and over and over again." Richard thought that was kind of cool. A rare compliment from the master.

The retreat began late one afternoon in the group room; there were about twelve "students." I was very uncomfortable not being in control and having no idea what I was doing. I was negative and cynical, using small talk and humor to deal with my uneasiness. Richard told us all to be quiet and after a few minutes declared that we were going on a rigorous hike in the foothills. We ended up on this cliff with a hundred-foot or so drop-off, and were told to go to the edge and put our toes over the edge. Some refused, for good reason, and were asked to leave the workshop. If you don't do all that's requested, you leave. It's that simple. I had no problem, as I like heights and was young enough to trust my balance.

We returned to the ranch and were sent into the desert in groups of three to sing until we had some sort of breakthrough. Now this felt real stupid. First of all, I can't sing well—in my band they would put a microphone in front of me but not plug it in! Second, what was this supposed to accomplish? There was no logic behind it. I was totally resisting this second exercise. But I went with my group, volunteered to go first, and sang what I remembered from Tim Buckley's song "Buzzin' Fly." Within two minutes I was sobbing for no reason I could identify. I still don't know what that was all about, but I do know it broke down most of my defenses.

Over the next nine days we did many unusual exercises. One was whirling, as in whirling dervishes. We were supposed to spin on the grass barefoot until we gave up control of everything. Two more people left the group for failing to participate in this exercise. I was doing my best, and Richard came over to me and said I was trying to control my being out of control. I spun like a maniac, fell down, and barfed on Richard's shoes.

We also did a lot of "Who are you?" exercises, fasted (no food or speech), and ended the fast with time in a sweat lodge at 4:00 AM. This was powerful stuff. And it worked: my ego was broken. But what now? The real necessity is learning to live with this awareness in the real world. This remains a challenge.

I participated in advanced retreats over the next few years—they helped me kick my drug habit and, later, provided the tools I needed to quit drinking—and this work was a major catalyst for change in my life.

18

FIGHTING FOR WOMEN WHO FIGHT BACK

While I was defending Benjamin Ng—and meditating my way toward sobriety—I was involved in two cases that might, given my counsel of Ted Bundy, surprise a lot of readers: Claudia Thacker and Ivy Kelly.

Claudia Thacker survived the Nazis. She survived an impoverished, asthmatic adolescence in post–World War II France. And for a long time Claudia Thacker survived Kenneth, the US Air Force officer who impressed her strict Catholic parents, won her hand in marriage, and brought her to the town of Port Orchard, Washington, some twenty miles southwest of Seattle.

For twenty years Claudia lived inside a nightmare, taking thrashings from Kenneth, who beat her before, during, and after intercourse, and who, as their four children matured—three daughters and one son—took to beating them too. By the mid-1970s a pattern had emerged: Kenneth would sulk in the basement for hours downing beers before climbing the stairs to unleash the breadth of his drunken rage on his family. Even the Port Orchard chief of police would later allow that his own kids, around the same age as Claudia's, used to note that the Thackers showed up to school spangled with bruises.

Claudia had few friends and no one to confide in. Kenneth forbade her from learning to drive, making outside connections—and any possible lifelines—nearly impossible to obtain. And she had to account for every penny: her husband would hand her a blank check and send her into the grocery store, and if the amount of the check stub didn't match the grocery receipt, she faced a pummeling. As things worsened she didn't even dare walk out to the mailbox, fearing Kenneth's reaction.

Then on Labor Day, September 5, 1977, Kenneth pushed her too far. He rose from the basement that afternoon after a long weekend of drinking and nattered on about, of all things, clothing. Claudia and the kids had recently bought school clothes. "Who buys sweaters in the middle of July?" he boomed, so inebriated that he didn't seem to know what month it was. When Claudia tried to calm him he kicked her, slammed her against the refrigerator, and then grabbed one of their daughters by the throat and threw her across the room. "I'm going to kill you all!"

Their son fled the house. The three girls escaped to their rooms.

As for Claudia, something in her changed. A sense of resolve flooded over her, and she ran to the master bedroom, to her husband's bedside table, to the one thing she could think of that would deliver her and her children from the nightmare.

Kenneth barged into their seventeen-year-old daughter Linda's room, back out into the hall, and then back toward Linda's room again. "I'm going to kill you!" he repeated.

The sound of gunfire. Claudia holding the pistol. Kenneth crumpling to the floor.

He died on the way to the hospital.

The verdict was swift: guilty of second-degree murder.

Out on her own recognizance, as her conviction was under appeal, Claudia worked at a floral shop and gained a sort of celebrity in the community. People, especially women, saw in her story something of themselves. "I'd have done the same thing Claudia did," an elderly businesswoman told *Seattle Times* reporter Janet Horne in an April 9, 1981, article. "Probably I'd kill for my grandchildren, too."

A local chapter of the National Organization for Women, or NOW, set up a legal fund and retained the services of John O'Connell, a former state attorney general (not the same John O'Connell who defended Ted Bundy in Utah). Evidence had been withheld from the first jury—a psychiatric evaluation that would have shed light on Claudia's state of mind at the time of the shooting. The state supreme court overturned the conviction. A new trial was set. And when the Northwest Women's Law Center requested that I represent Claudia, I gladly accepted.

In March 1981, three and a half years after Kenneth Thacker's death, and after numerous pretrial motions, Judge

J. W. Hamilton allowed us to present evidence of the battered woman syndrome to the jury. The condition is complex and in some ways counterintuitive, as battered women can be strong individuals on the outside. It's characterized by "learned helplessness" brought on by many factors, all involving the loss of individual power and self-worth. Those who abuse their partners (there are battered men also) take control of all aspects of that partner's life. They control all the money and must give permission for the partner to leave the house or to have a particular friend. The goal is to isolate the spouse. All this is critical for jury members to understand, lest they assume the battered spouse could have walked out at any time. They cannot. The syndrome traps them.

I also showed the jury charts and maps of the Thacker home on the day of the shooting to dispute the prosecution's contention that Kenneth was shot from behind. "Look at the path of the bullet," the *Seattle Times* quoted me telling the jury. "Now unless he's walking down the hallway *sideways*, bullets don't go like that. But if he's standing over Linda, that's what would have happened."

The elected prosecutor in the county, known for his buffoonery, had said that if Mrs. Thacker got away with the crime, it would be "open season" on husbands. Well, she did get away with it. The jury found her not guilty in less than one hour, which included a lunch break. The jury also awarded her attorney fees, a novel procedure in Washington State reserved for those who've been found to be wrongfully prosecuted in a self-defense case.

Like Kenneth Thacker, Jack Kelly, fifty-nine, was a mean drunk. On Saturday, August 30, 1980, he started early, draining all the booze in the house before stamping off to the liquor store to replenish.

He returned late in the afternoon, stumbling into the kitchen, where Ivy, sixty, was placing in the freezer the apple pies she'd made and was about to make jelly with the apple peelings. She had had three kids, now grown and with children of their own, before she married Jack four years earlier. He beat her regularly, one time so badly that she required hospitalization.

"Have a drink with me," he implored.

They sat down for a drink. Then, inexplicably, Jack grabbed Ivy's full glass and poured it on her head. He stammered an apology and served her another round. But he had *the look*.

Slurred speech, glassy eyes—Ivy knew the signs. A beating was imminent.

He stepped outside with some tools to do repairs around the house, then came roaring back inside. "I'm going to kill you, you witch!" he screamed, blocking the only exit.

Ivy retreated to the coffee table where Jack kept his gun in a drawer. She raised the weapon and aimed, hoping Jack would back down. When he didn't Ivy pulled the trigger, and Jack collapsed.

Despite evidence that her husband had banged her up in the past, a Snohomish County Superior Court jury found Ivy guilty of second-degree murder, and she faced a twenty-year prison sentence. The problem was that in many aspects of her life Ivy was the epitome of a powerful woman. She was even a bush pilot in the Alaskan wilderness. In rebuttal to the defense case the prosecution was allowed to put on evidence that Ivy had aggressive exchanges with neighbors and, on one occasion, went after Jack with a shovel, banging on the back door with it, trying to get back into the house, where Jack was armed with a gun.

The Northwest Women's Law Center brought me in to work on Ivy's appeal. I argued that such specific instances of prior conduct were not admissible as relevant to disprove self-defense. (Even if they were relevant, they were much more prejudicial than relevant.) No luck. In December 1982, the state court of appeals upheld Snohomish County's decision.

We then took our case to the state supreme court, which heard it in September 1983. By then we'd refined the strategy: When a man kills another man in a bar fight in self-defense, that defendant's character isn't questioned in court. So why was Ivy Kelly's?

This time the judges agreed, eight to one, reversing Ivy's murder conviction and prompting a new trial. In its ruling the court explained, "Petitioner was on trial for the murder of her husband. She was not on trial for yelling at her neighbors or for beating on her own door with a shovel."

This case was even more important than Claudia Thacker's, as it limited what evidence could be used, in any instance, to refute certain character evidence. *State v. Kelly* is often cited as the seminal case placing limits on the admission of supposed acts of prior misconduct.

The charges were dropped before Ivy's second trial was scheduled to begin in 1985, and she went on to live a productive life, active in various women's advocacy groups. She would often stop by my office when in Seattle and would try to talk me into going with her to Alaska for a plane ride, even though she was too old to maintain her pilot's license. She passed away a few years ago, well into her nineties.

Claudia, meanwhile, went on to have a rewarding career working for the federal government. I get a Christmas card from her and her kids every year.

And yet these cases confused a lot of people. Here I was, an early advocate for abused women, breaking new judicial ground and bringing attention to a syndrome that was only beginning to be understood, while at the same time famous for defending Ted Bundy, the most notorious killer of women. For me it was easy. The system was taking aim at both, disregarding fairness and the law. Besides, I was done with Ted Bundy.

Too bad he wasn't done with me.

19

THE EXECUTION OF TED BUNDY

After his trials in 1979 and 1980 I received periodic letters and Christmas cards from Ted and had some personal interaction with his new wife, Carole, as well as their daughter, Rosebud. (Carole, a friend from his days in Seattle, had testified during the Florida trial and was on the witness stand when Ted asked her to marry him. Their daughter's conception has long been the focus of bizarre speculation; a guard would later claim that Ted had smuggled a semen-filled condom into the death row visitation room and passed it to Carole mouth-to-mouth via a kiss, and that Carole quickly repaired to a fertility clinic to be artificially inseminated with Ted's sperm.)

It's chilling to me that no one else seems to have made the connection that Ted had forever tainted his daughter by calling her Rosebud, the name he used as the fictitious police officer in the Carol DaRonch kidnapping and when he called me from jail in Florida.

Although I hadn't heard much from Ted for a few years, I did get a letter from Carole in January 1980. It was typewritten and apparently designed to keep me in the loop with Ted and solicit my assistance in the Kimberly Leach murder trial and Ted's appeals.

> Happy New Year, tan person [she knew I had returned from Mexico recently].
>
> Que Pasa?
>
> Enough chitchat. Writing you seems novel. Bear with my typing/it is much better than the script. Bunny [Ted] professes ability to decipher Egyptian hieroglyphics after these many years of illegible missiles. Our boy isn't doing real well, but I think it is appropriate, and even beneficial. He came back up after the Miami trial, and shut off. Never any good way to deal with the shit because eventually It Will Out. . . . It will get better again. This has happened before. He will resort to dreams of his personal favorite solution for a while until something happens. Then he will bounce back . . .
>
> Listen, again/there is no intention of you doing it for free. It would be (get it?/would be) helpful if you would put your Parker to paper and roughly estimate expenses, fees, retainers and all that jazz.
>
> I know that it is hard, but give the thing a whirl. Don't pay any attention to Theo [Ted], about this money stuff. He isn't in a position to fuss about it at the moment. We have kept him mildly uninformed because of internal problems.
>
> His attorney friend in Seattle, Marlin, didn't work out (it is a long and boring story) with the money, and Ted

has been kept out because he doesn't have so many friends that he can afford to lose one. Or the illusion of one. . . .

Y'all take care now/I must go pick up Jamie [her son] up [*sic*] from his martial arts class. Again and again, thank you for your help. I know you were busy, probably not because of your talent, but rather your looks. But busy you are, and there it is.

It is much to your credit that you put up with our hysteria on top of all the legal advice. You are the only attorney that I don't talk—the only attorney that I don't talk about behind his back, if that is any repayment.

Cordially,
"Bubbles"

I later declined to help, as the whole Bundy affair began to negatively affect my personal life, and I just wanted nothing more to do with him. I let Carole and Ted know that I was not interested in assisting him legally and was sticking to the position I took, along with Millard Farmer, in the holding cell in Tallahassee, that if Ted wanted to die, I was not going to assist him.

My last contact with Ted of any consequence was in October 1984, in the midst of another rash of serial murders in the Pacific Northwest. The Green River Task Force, which included members of the Ted Task Force, had been formed to find a prolific killer of prostitutes active in the Seattle area in the 1980s and '90s. He was dubbed the Green River Killer because he had disposed of some of the victims near the Green River, which flows through Seattle's suburbs.

I received a letter from Ted Bundy from death row in Starke, Florida.

> I have a favor to ask of you. Would you mind taking the enclosed letter I have written to someone associated with the Green River Task Force who has some sense and can be trusted to take the right steps to see that the letter both receives proper consideration and remains confidential? . . .
>
> There are a number of reasons why I offer my help to the Task Force at this time. . . . I would like to figure out what makes the Green River guy tick, and I figure I have as good a chance of doing that as anyone on the Task Force. And I also think that the time seems right in some inexplicable sort of way, and I find myself saying, quote, "Why not put some of your knowledge and unique perspective to use. It could be interesting."
>
> I don't fancy myself playing detective, but I will bet I can play the man or men they are looking for better than any of them.
>
> Please let me know you received this and what, if anything, happened when you passed it along.
>
> Thank you for your help. Take care of yourself.
>
> Peace.
>
> Ted
>
> P.S. And remember, you can arrange to reach me by phone, if you wish.

Ted's letter is stunning in his clothed admissions of guilt, which I believe he only felt comfortable making to me because of our interactions in the cell in Miami. In other words, Ted knew I knew he was guilty and the mind-boggling extent of his crimes. Without directly stating that in the letter, it is obvious from his assertion that he wanted to assist the Green River Task Force because of his "unique perspective." I find his statement about "playing the man or men they are looking for better than any of them" chilling.

Investigators would ultimately identify the Green River Killer as a truck driver named Gary Ridgway, who admitted to killing more than forty women. At the time Ted wrote this letter Ridgway was still at large, and I believed Ted's motive was simply to find another avenue to prolong his life, as the imposition of electrocution seemed likely within the next few years. Yes, Ted had a death wish years earlier when he turned down the plea bargain, but the reality of his imminent execution seemed to be setting in, and his survival instincts, I believe, had kicked in. If he could convince the task force that he could be of assistance, it might result in sparing his life, at least for a few more years. I do not believe in any way that his motives were altruistic.

Interestingly, one of the task force detectives, Robert Keppel—the same detective who tried to get me to provide evidence against Ted back in 1976—later wrote a book about the Green River Killer, which included a lot of information about his investigation of Ted Bundy.

Keep in mind that neither the Ted Task Force nor the Green River Task Force really solved either of those crimes. Keppel's book was later turned into a movie. And in the book and film he claims that Ted Bundy sent this letter to him directly. He says he found it sitting on his kitchen table after arriving home one evening.

False. I delivered this letter to the task force—see appendix B, page 232—and their initial response was laughter, for understandable reasons. They were not interested in any "assistance" from Ted and made that very clear to me. I later conveyed this to Ted via a telephone call. (As far as I know, they made no contact with Ted as a result of the letter. Their last contact with him was days before his execution, when he was frantically trying to blame pornography and alcohol for his behavior and the authorities thought he might come clean regarding all of his crimes if he spoke with Seattle detectives.)

There are similarities between mass murderers but very few, I believe, between Ted Bundy and Gary Ridgway. Ridgway, also a sociopath, preyed only on prostitutes, and sex was always part of his crimes. As we know, Ted preyed on beautiful, naive, fresh-faced college women who all had a similar appearance. And he was interested more in playing his game of control than in sex. (Ridgway avoided the death penalty by assisting the authorities in solving some open cases. I met with him at his request and told him he had a great team of attorneys, led by the late Tony Savage, and he should keep the team. It was Tony and other gifted attorneys who really did the impossible by saving Ridgway from the death penalty.)

Prior to his execution on January 24, 1989, there was a frenzy of activity surrounding Ted: various police authorities seeking last-minute confessions (and the locations of victims' bodies) and Ted's on-camera interview with Evangelical Christian psychologist James Dobson. Ted was desperately trying to postpone his execution by revealing, for the first time, that his motivation and illness were the result of addiction to pornography as a teenager and young adult.

This, from what Ted told me himself, was completely untrue. However, it did result in a lot of attention concerning pornography and Ted's stated attempt to provide himself as a "study" so society could learn of the evils of pornography. It was simply Ted's way of postponing his execution, as the evil part of him wanted to continue to live.

I had little contact with Ted after calling him about the Green River Task Force, although I continued to receive birthday and Christmas cards.

He did call me approximately one month prior to the final execution date and asked if I would be a witness to his execution. I declined immediately.

The evening before the execution, I spent an hour on the local CBS affiliate, KIRO Television, in a dialogue with then local anchorperson Aaron Brown, who later became an anchor for CNN. It was, for television, an intimate moment, as I had known Aaron for a long time, and we were discussing the dynamics of Ted's situation and the frenzy surrounding his execution the next morning in Starke.

Local radio stations in Florida, as was the custom, were playing the sounds of frying bacon, which was to simulate the sound of the electric chair, and joyfully calling for Ted's execution.

There were hundreds of people at the prison awaiting and cheering for his death, and a few anti–death penalty protesters. The parking lot was full of satellite news vans beaming live coverage.

I left the studio in Seattle at approximately 11:00 PM and went to a friend's house, a kind and nurturing person, and woke up the next morning to learn that Ted had indeed been executed.

20

PRESUMED GUILTY

In the winter of 1991, two years after the State of Florida executed Ted, I sat in a darkened theater on Bainbridge Island, Washington. The movie was *The Silence of the Lambs*. Jonathan Demme's film about the crime-solving serial killer Hannibal Lecter is pretty tame by today's standards, but it was hard-going for me from the start.

By then I had represented Benjamin Ng and countless other murderers—including, of course, the most notorious serial killer of all time. To see Hollywood turn these men into antiheros—a trend that has continued with shows like *Dexter* and *Hannibal*—appalled me.

I never made it to the end of the film. After a few revelations about, say, Lecter dining on some guy's liver with a side of "fava beans and a nice chianti," or Buffalo Bill skinning women alive, I was out. I squeezed along the aisle and stepped outside the theater. I felt sick to my stomach—just as I had my last time in Ted Bundy's cell.

People often ask me, "If you're so disgusted with these acts of evil, why are you a criminal defense lawyer?"

My answer is that I am in this line of work to do good. I saved Benjamin Ng's life not because I thought Benjamin Ng was virtuous but because I believe killing is wrong, whether it's committed by an individual or sponsored by the state.

I'm also all too aware of how fallible our system is, that it can and does charge and convict the wrong people. I'd like to talk about three such defendants: David Kunze, Dr. James Stansfield, and Donna Rodriguez.

David Kunze had been convicted of the 1994 aggravated first-degree murder of his ex-wife's fiancé, based only on an alleged ear print left at the crime scene. This was the first case in the United States where the state used this sort of forensic science, ear prints, to gain a conviction. The expert the state had used was a high school–educated policeman from the Netherlands who carried a rubber ear around in his pocket. He claimed that "no two ears are alike" and that the smudge left at the murder scene was in fact a print of David's right ear. I represented David during the appeal process, and, finding the evidence faulty, a three-judge state court of appeals overturned the conviction in 1999. A new trial was set.

For the retrial, in 2001, the state elected to make a jailhouse informant the meat of its case. This informant was a convicted sex offender who was provided favors by the state for testifying that David confessed to him in jail. Unknown to the state, I obtained this informant's complete prison file, which included details of his proclivities. It seems he liked to have sex with cows. At trial I asked him if it was untrue that he had sex with cows. He became indignant and said, "No, calves!"

The judge had to take a recess to quiet the laughter in the courtroom, including the jury box. Later on in the trial I discovered that the trial attorney for the prosecution had been giving money to this informant and failed to inform me, as required by law. The trial judge dismissed the case for prosecution misconduct, and David was freed. This case illustrates how easy a person's freedom can be taken away with bogus and purchased evidence. Sadly, it happens every day.

Junk science is a real threat to our liberties. Juries tend to give much weight to testimony clothed in scientific terms, the so-called CSI effect. Another of my cases revolved around the state's use of an expert to re-create an auto accident using a computer program called PC Crash. I moved to exclude the evidence, calling it a "cartoon," but the trial judge, a real idiot, was apparently impressed by cartoons and allowed the evidence in the trial. After conviction, the court of appeals held that there was no scientific evidence supporting the validity of the computer program and tossed the homicide conviction out. My client was able to plead guilty to a DUI and avoided a homicide conviction. A sad note was that two other individuals, whose attorneys did not challenge this evidence, were convicted based on similar cartoons. The so-called expert was later sued for his willing participation in this farce.

In 1990 James Stansfield, a retired general practitioner in Quincy, Washington, was accused of killing his wife, Patricia Stansfield, and a neighbor, Frederick Smith. The rumor was that Dr. Stansfield was having an affair with Smith's wife and wanted his own wife and Fred out of the way.

Patricia died in her sleep, apparently after she stopped breathing. Fred died in a car crash. The local police suspected that Stansfield had poisoned them both. But the case was a mess from the start. The coroner had dementia. He was prone to non sequitur recitations from *Hamlet*, and he embalmed one of the bodies *before* the autopsy. Fred Smith's body wasn't buried for ten days, because no one could find his hands. They were eventually found in a cooler in the coroner's car.

I was able to get the charges dropped after pointing out all the holes in the state's case, including, most significantly, how badly the Washington State Patrol Crime Lab had handled the toxicology investigation.

The day we won the case we celebrated on Stansfield's farm. I was taking a shower there before the party when the shower curtain flew open. The doctor stood in front of me, and I tried to cover my wet, naked body. He grumbled "Here!" and handed me a triple bourbon.

In March 1995 I took a phone call from a woman named Jean Wake of Wenatchee, a town in eastern Washington. Jean told me that a woman who worked for her, Donna Rodriguez, had been arrested and charged with multiple counts of child molestation and child rape. It was, according to Jean, connected to what prosecutors were calling "a child sex ring" known as the Circle.

I agreed to represent Donna and, with my talented investigator Chris Beck, began looking into the allegations. I am confident you, the reader, will be shocked and perhaps disbelieving of the facts we uncovered with the help of some other attorneys and the national media, particularly Dorothy Rabinowitz of the *Wall Street Journal*, Tom Grant of the local CBS affiliate in Spokane, and John Larson of NBC's *Dateline*.

The facts were that two teen sisters, foster children of Robert and Luci Perez, had made a series of escalating sex abuse allegations involving, in the end, over thirty adults, one being Donna Rodriguez. Most of the events involved members of a small, lower-class church run by an ex-biker, Pastor Robert Roberson, and his wife, Connie.

But here is the beginning of the unbelievable part: Robert Perez was the sex crimes investigator for the Wenatchee Police Department, and he was actively and aggressively investigating the charges (most of which were unbelievable) made by his own foster daughters. He charged some individuals with over six thousand counts each of rape or molestation. His investigation was blindly accepted by the prosecutor, the chief of police, and most important, the only newspaper in town, the *Wenatchee World*. You would think that any reasonable prosecutor would be greatly concerned about a policeman charging one person with over six thousand counts of child abuse. Same with the local newspaper and the local judges. No, the town's power brokers circled the wagons.

Detective Perez was a zealot. If you can imagine a blond George Costanza wearing ugly short-sleeved shirts, pants hiked over his belly fat, and handcuffs and a 9 millimeter always visible on his belt, you get the picture. To demonstrate his power and insanity, if you questioned his tactics, you would become a suspect in his investigation. A social worker and a reporter who went public with complaints about Perez were soon accused of being part of the Circle.

The original allegations by the foster children escalated from a few supposed perpetrators to the involvement of Pastor Roberson's entire church, where, according to Perez, there were rampant sex and rituals on the altar involving intercourse with children as young as six. There were, according to Perez, orgies in the basement of the church involving masturbation and the insertion of objects into the victims, and at another location, where the same participants allegedly wore dark robes and sunglasses.

Such escalation of details is typically a telltale sign of a false allegation. There has, in fact, never been a proven "sex ring" in the United States, despite public opinion—and hysteria—to the contrary. It is also true that very few child sex abusers are female, yet about half of Detective Perez's suspects were women.

Through intimidation and outright lies, Perez secured other witnesses to support the allegations of his foster daughters. Many of the defendants and coerced witnesses were uneducated, could not read or write, and/or had IQs of seventy or below. No matter to Perez. He even had illiterate suspects sign confessions, which he claimed they read before they signed. This didn't seem to bother the judges though, who supported the prosecutions in every way possible. It seemed like the whole system in Wenatchee had lost its mind.

At one point we found a document from an old case in which the police chief had been critical of Perez for, among other things, "targeting people" and intimidation. The *Wenatchee World* ran a story about how inappropriate it was for us to use such information. No mention of the substance of the complaints against good ole Bob Perez.

He, the other cops, and the social workers never recorded interviews, and destroyed their notes, leaving only their versions of what the witnesses had said. (One social worker complained and within one week was charged with crimes related to the sex ring.)

The worst of the corruption came from the public defenders. Most public defenders are honorable, hardworking advocates. In Wenatchee they were hacks. Many pled their clients guilty with no investigation.

So into this scene I walked with my trusted investigator. We smelled a corrupt prosecution and a broken system. We were the first team not beholden to the local system. We put in over two hundred hours investigating the case and saw all the flaws. We discovered that Perez and a social worker had taken one of his foster daughters on a drive past every house where members of the church lived, and according to Perez and the social worker, his foster daughter picked out every house of church members where rituals and abuse occurred. This later became know in our investigation as the Parade of Homes. We learned that Perez would punish his foster children, even physically, if they were reluctant to testify.

My team realized that most of the local public defenders were conduits for information to the prosecutor's office. As a result we did not share our investigation with these attorneys.

On one occasion there was a group meeting of all the defense lawyers involved, twenty or more. But we kept our investigation to ourselves and later learned that one of the public defenders was reporting directly to the prosecutor and Perez.

Donna Rodriguez, our client, became a defendant through a pattern of intimidation tactics Perez used on others. She was a member of Pastor Roberson's church and therefore, in Perez's mind, a likely member of the sex ring. He went to Donna's daughter's school and called her out for a six-hour interrogation. He told Donna's daughter that if she did not implicate her mother and assist his investigation, he would have Donna arrested in five minutes. The daughter insisted that she had never been molested and Donna did not even know some of the people Perez was talking about. Finally, on the threat of having her mother arrested, the daughter said "Whatever" to Perez. Donna was arrested and taken to jail February 2, 1995, and charged with several counts of child rape and molestation. What Perez did not know was that Donna's daughter recanted the day after and did so on camera.

We interviewed Perez's foster daughters, whose story fell apart, and we developed damaging information about Perez and demonstrated the absurdity of all the allegations. All charges against Donna were dismissed on August 8, 1995. Within months the entire story collapsed. Most of the accused were released without prejudice, and Perez's "sex ring" was deemed a fiction.

21

COLTON HARRIS-MOORE

By the time I got a call from journalist Bob Friel in June 2010, teenager Colton Harris-Moore had become a part of local folklore. The Island County, Washington, Sheriff's Department suspected Harris-Moore in hundreds of burglaries on his native Camano Island and surrounding islands, including the theft of cars and airplanes. When deputies found footprints at the crime scenes—barefoot prints—the media latched onto a legend. The so-called Barefoot Bandit, still at large after a two-year crime spree, was a source of international fascination.

Friel had written a profile of Harris-Moore for *Outside* magazine and was maintaining a blog about the young pilot's exploits, *Outlaws and Outcasts*—a blog, it was assumed, Colton was reading. Friel asked me if he could announce on the blog that I was willing to represent Colton once he was in custody and include my cell phone number so Colton could reach me.

"Why not?" I said. "Do it."

Later that day Friel posted the following:

> Here's a big news flash: John Henry Browne, a criminal defense attorney who many people consider the best in the entire state of Washington, says that he's willing to represent Colton Harris-Moore.
>
> Colt, I don't know if you realize the significance of this, but it's huge. Look Browne up . . . and then call him on his cell. . . . Anything you say to him or ask him about is 100% confidential.
>
> We know you could run forever, Colt. The problem with that, though, is exactly that: You'll be running forever, always looking over your shoulder. Now, however, you know you can end this on your terms and have your own "dream team" lawyer to give you the best defense possible.
>
> You've still got choices, and this seems like an easy one.

A day or so later I received a call from Pam Kohler, Colton's mother. She said the family had no money to pay me for my services. I said, "Fine, send me a dollar." And she did.

My office got to work on the case, and as I learned more about my young, elusive client, I not only grew to like him but also came to realize the deck had been stacked against him from the very beginning.

When Pam Kohler was pregnant in late 1990 and early 1991, she smoked constantly and drank heavily at least once a week, joining her brother at the bar and throwing back drinks until she could barely walk. After her son Colton was born, in March 1991, she continued to drink. She was a mean drunk, prone to telling her son things like "I wish you had been born dead."

Raised by Pam and the various, often abusive men who came in and out of her life, Colton lived in constant fear. And hunger. Pam rarely kept food in the single-wide, two-bedroom trailer parked on five acres in a remote part of Camano Island. In elementary school Colton started to break into nearby homes, where he'd go straight to the kitchen and stock up on food. "I only took small food items," he later told my investigator, "to avoid suspicion of a break-in so that I could come back the next time I was hungry." At age thirteen Colton broke into his school to pilfer candy—and was immediately caught while slinking out of the building.

The deputy decided not to arrest him and instead admonished him on the evils of theft and drove him home. But the incident further cemented what had become, since he was a child, a distrustful, contentious relationship between Colton and the Island County Sheriff's Department. When Colton received a new bike as a gift—one of the few possessions he ever had—deputies were convinced he stole it, and escorted him and the new bike home, where they confronted Pam. From her they learned, to their embarrassment, that something nice actually belonged to Colton.

The bicycle was an anomaly in a childhood marked by want, abuse, and hunger. Child Protective Services was called on Colton's behalf twelve times before he turned fifteen years old. No real action was ever taken, and he was never removed from his home.

By then Colton was ready to take matters into his own hands. In August 2006 he ran away. He roamed the island like a ghost, living in the woods and breaking into vacant vacation homes to appropriate electronics—laptops, cell phones, cameras—and food. He evaded sheriff's deputies for six months before they caught him.

The state sentenced him to three years of incarceration and placed him in Green Hill School, a maximum-security detention center in Chehalis, Washington, reserved for the worst juvenile offenders. Six months later he was transferred to the relatively posh Griffin Home, a transitional housing unit in a Seattle suburb, with a great record for reforming its occupants. At first Colton was excited about Griffin, because it looked like a shot at a real education, one that might even allow him to study aviation and help fulfill his dream of becoming a pilot. He was deflated when a counselor told him, "You will never be a pilot." In late April 2008 Colton slipped out a window and escaped.

Here's what got me: Griffin was, by all measures, the best place Colton could have served out his sentence. But he ran, and looking at his case file, I couldn't for the life of me understand why.

After he left Griffin, Colton stole—and then crashed—a Mercedes and disappeared into the woods on Camano. For the next two years he was an apparition. People reported seeing him all over the islands.

In November 2008 he took a single-engine Cessna—after teaching himself how to fly by reading the owner's manual—and got as far as Yakima County, three hundred miles away in eastern Washington, before crashing. He emerged from the wreckage and hiked some fifty miles into the hamlet of White Swan, Washington, jacked a car, and rolled down to California, where he connected with a friend and cooled his heels.

Back on Camano Island nine months later, the stealing spree continued. And the legend grew. A Colton Harris-Moore Facebook page collected more than forty thousand fans. A screen-printer in Seattle produced a T-shirt with Colton's face below the words MOMMA TRIED (a nod to the song "Mama Tried" by Merle Haggard) and said he was donating some of the proceeds toward Colton's legal defense fund. (Neither Colton nor I ever saw a dollar of it!)

But while my client had allies in Seattle, and all over the world for that matter, the locals he grew up around—particularly those whom he'd allegedly stolen from—considered him a menace. One San Juan Islander sold coffee mugs, T-shirts, and other paraphernalia that featured my client as a hapless delinquent. Sample T-shirt: COLTON HARRIS-MOORE, TURN YOURSELF IN AND WE'LL GIVE YOU THE SECOND HALF OF THE FLIGHT MANUAL, YOU KNOW, THE PART ABOUT *LANDING*. He said he'd donate 25 percent of his proceeds toward a reward for anyone with information that resulted in Colton's arrest.

My client climbed into his second airplane on September 11, 2009, in Friday Harbor, took off, and headed for nearby Canada. But remembering he'd left his iPod on Orcas Island (what can I say, he was eighteen and not good at prioritizing), he circled back and landed on Orcas to retrieve it. There he stole a boat and headed for the US mainland, where he pinched a car, making his way to Bonners Ferry, Idaho. Another stolen plane took him back to Washington, as far as Granite Falls, before he crash-landed.

He returned to Camano, where he lived in the woods and continued to break into homes. When he'd sneak a call to his mother on a stolen cell phone, she was anything but helpful. Rather than pleading with him to turn himself in, she encouraged him to run, at one point saying, "You will probably be killed if you get caught."

It's important to point out that Colton was never violent, that although he started to keep a handgun close by for protection, he in fact avoided violent confrontation at every turn. During one incident, as he pilfered food from a refrigerator, an old man walked into the kitchen and issued a simple "Hi." My client, clearly more frightened than the old man, bolted from the house.

In June 2010, right around the time I heard from journalist Bob Friel and Colton's mother, Colton fled across the country, stealing cars and boats along the way. In South Dakota he broke into what he thought was a vacant home to do laundry. When he heard the owners, a man and woman, come home around 3:00 AM, he locked the door. At the sound of the lock the woman shrieked and the man broke down the door and chased Colton, who called out, "I am trying to get out of your house." The couple decided to let Colton leave, and he slipped out of a window in the basement.

On July 4, feeling the pressure of what had become a nationwide manhunt, Colton stole a Cessna in Bloomington, Indiana. He flew it more than a thousand miles before crash-landing in the Bahamas. Seven days later, after a high-speed boat chase that involved authorities opening fire on Colton's boat, my client was caught and arrested.

I met him for the first time about a month later. How to describe him? Colton is an unusually bright young man. Tall, like me, but quiet and soft spoken (not like me). We liked each other instantly. He also warmed up to another lawyer in my firm, Emma Scanlan. As far as I could tell, we were the first adults Colton had trusted in his life.

He was charged with nearly seventy crimes in six states and two different countries. Prosecutors wanted him in prison for twenty years. Emma and I were determined to see that didn't happen.

In court the San Juan prosecutor made a fool of himself. He said to Island County Superior Court judge Vickie Churchill—and I'm paraphrasing here—"The victims on Orcas Island were not just regular people. These were really substantial people of wealth and power."

I couldn't believe it. You don't say, "Oh, the victims are wealthy; therefore it means more!" I remember whispering to Colton, "He just shot himself in the foot." That drew a smile from Colton, a big smile—the first I'd ever seen on his face.

The other prosecutor continued with the foot shooting. He told the judge—again, I'm paraphrasing—"The newspaper headlines tomorrow should read JUDGE IMPOSES HARSH SENTENCE ON COLTON HARRIS-MOORE." Basically he was telling the judge what she should do. A big no-no.

Fortunately, the judge saw in Colton what Emma and I saw: a gifted young man who had a hard childhood and had made some big mistakes. The fact that no one was hurt during his two-and-a-half-year crime spree worked in his favor, but there was also his *Colt-ness*, which I can only describe as fierce independence.

When the judge asked him why, back in 2008, he had fled from the relatively comfortable confines of the Griffin Home halfway house, Colton said he wanted to go back to Green Hill School, the maximum-security juvenile detention center. This stunned the courtroom, me included.

"Why on earth would you want to go back there?" Judge Churchill asked.

"Because Griffin was trying to change who I am," Colton answered.

We're talking about someone who was seventeen years old at the time of his escape. (I wish I had been as confident in who I was at that age.)

Emma and I were able to get the prosecutors on board with a deal: All the charges against Colton would be consolidated. All money Colton made from an impending movie deal—which he didn't want a dime of—would go toward restitution to the victims of his crimes.

Before she leveled the sentence—less than seven years—it was Judge Churchill's turn to stun the courtroom. She detailed all she had learned via reports submitted to the court about Colton's rotten upbringing. And then she said:

> I was struck that I could have been reading a history of a mass murderer or someone who indiscriminately killed without any remorse. I could have been reading about a drug addicted, alcoholic, abusive young man who followed in the path of his mother. Yet I was not reading that story. That is the triumph of the human spirit and the triumph of Colton Harris-Moore.

Indeed, Colton, one of my favorite clients to date, truly is a triumph. Another attorney and I were able to connect him with an engineer at Boeing who now meets with him in prison once a month. Colton is studying aeronautical engineering. He's twenty-five now. He'll be free soon. A movie about his life is in development. (Robert Zemeckis is rumored to direct.) Per our agreement, all proceeds will go to those Colton stole from.

In his very last court appearance, in May 2013, for a minor matter related to his crimes in Skagit County, Washington, my client wrote a statement for the judge that, two years into his sentence, shined with optimism:

> The past is a story absolutely separate from the future. The past holds experiences and lessons I'll learn from for the rest of my life, but my future is precisely what I make it. If there is any truth I've learned, it is that absolutely anything is possible. When this is over and I regain my freedom, I will bring everything I am working towards into reality. I am working with amazing people.

On the last line he added, "And I will have a beautiful life."

22

A MASSACRE IN KANDAHAR

In November 2012 I boarded a rickety blue-and-white 727 and flew two and a half hours from Dubai to Kandahar City. The plane, built in 1967, seemed held together by duct tape (as many of the seats literally were). On board were members of the military and the CIA as well as a few fellow civilians. When we touched down in Kandahar an explosion ripped the sky next to the runway. The Taliban, I later learned, had fired rockets at gas tanks near the airfield.

Welcome to Afghanistan.

I had come to the heart of the so-called war on terror for a preliminary hearing for my latest client: Sgt. Robert Bales, accused of a one-man raid on two Afghan villages. Military investigators said that in the early morning hours of March 11, 2012, Sergeant Bales slaughtered sixteen innocent civilians, most of them women and children (some as young as two years old). The villages were a couple miles from a Special Forces outpost—a forward operating base, or FOB—in the middle of the Panjwayi District, birthplace of the Taliban.

Retained by Bales's family back in Washington State, where he had been stationed at Joint Base Lewis-McChord, near Tacoma, I'd been waging a case in the media since almost immediately after my client was charged.

"If Sergeant Bales did this," I told reporters, "and I do mean *if*, then we are responsible. We the American people made Sergeant Bales." I believed that Bales, on his fourth deployment when the massacre occurred, suffered from posttraumatic stress disorder (PTSD) and that his country had done little to help his mental health. I believed that after over more than a decade of wars in the Middle East, we were putting all of our soldiers at risk. And I wanted to put the *wars* on trial.

Now here I was stepping off an aircraft that would never pass inspection back home and onto the Kandahar airfield. There I met my military lawyer counterpart, Capt. Matthew Aiesi—the spitting image of Matt Lauer, by the way—and my bodyguard for the trip, Staff Sgt. Brittany Brinker, a paralegal specialist. Armed and sheathed in body armor, they brought new meaning to the term *defense attorneys*.

I too was soon covered in body armor and ushered into a Blackhawk helicopter, bound for FOB Camp Nathan Smith—named after a Canadian soldier killed in a friendly fire incident in which a US Air National Guard F-16 pilot dropped a laser-guided, half-ton bomb on a group of Canadians conducting a training exercise.

I could barely sit up straight in the cramped helicopter. *No wonder the military has height restrictions.* During the twenty-minute ride to Camp Nathan Smith I listened to Leonard Cohen's "Hallelujah" on repeat on my iPod headphones. Looking around I saw the look of genuine fear on the .50-caliber machine gun operators hanging out the Blackhawk doors on both sides. Neither they nor the pilots ever smiled. I could feel the fear of all those on board and had flashbacks to how deep and genuine my life had been—how blessed. If this was it and I died here, I thought, then this was it.

At the base we would spend the next week in preliminary hearings and interviewing witnesses—many surviving family members—to the massacre in which Bales was the military's only suspect. I was issued a light Kevlar vest, heavy Kevlar vest (fifty pounds), helmet (twenty pounds), and—what I'm sure must have violated a regulation or four—loaded M-16 rifle and 9-millimeter handgun. In a photo taken at the time, with all that armor and my white beard, I look like a militarized Santa Claus.

Five foot one, *maybe* a hundred pounds, Staff Sgt. Brittany Brinker took her job as my bodyguard very seriously. We'd walk into, say, the commissary, frequented by both US and Afghan soldiers, and she'd eye the place like a cat. She even pissed off a major who greatly outranked her when she told him, "Sir, you cannot bring your bag into the commissary." She was and is my hero, all five foot one of her.

Captain Aiesi and I shared quarters. And by *quarters* I mean a converted shipping container, a cramped metal rectangle that could barely fit our bunk beds and gear. The stencils on our compartment read, RIFLE SIX and RIFLE SEVEN. I was designated Rifle Six, and Aiesi was Rifle Seven. For some long-standing army reason, this made me the big cheese, as Rifle Six is the leader in any group.

A few yards outside our door sat a cement bunker made of what looked like oversize parking blocks jigsawed together into a lean-to. They were scattered all over Camp Nathan Smith. If the base suspected an incoming Taliban rocket, a siren would blare and I'd have exactly forty-seven seconds to get from wherever I was (asleep on my bunk, taking care of business in the porta potty) to one of the cement bunkers.

It happened three times during my stay.

Let me back up. Eight months earlier, March 11, 2012, and some fifty miles to the southwest, according to my client and two witnesses—Staff Sgt. Jason McLaughlin and Cpl. David Godwin—Robert Bales sat on a bed in McLaughlin's room. He poured Jack Daniels from a Dasani water bottle into a Diet Coke. On the television flickered the image of actor Denzel Washington laying waste to kidnappers in Mexico City. In the film *Man on Fire* Washington plays a former CIA operative who goes on a killing spree/rescue mission after the nine-year-old daughter of the man who hired him to prevent such a kidnapping is abducted.

Bales had just returned from guard duty atop Village Support Platform (VSP) Belambay, temporary home of the Third Special Forces Group's Second Battalion and army support troops—including Bales—who were there to provide locals a safe alternative to the Taliban.

On guard duty on the roof Bales had told another soldier that he'd spotted two lights flashing in the nearby villages of Naja Bien and Alikozai. He reportedly observed the lights flashing for fifteen minutes and said he thought they might be a sequence of signals between Taliban insurgents in the two villages.

Now, back in the soldiers' quarters, as the whiskey took hold and the violence on the TV screen played out, Bales thought about those lights and about the incident five days earlier when a fellow soldier lost his left leg to an IED (improvised explosive device). Bales believed Special Forces weren't doing enough to tamp down the enemy.

What the US government says the thirty-eight-year-old father of two did next is more shocking than any event from any case I've ever had. (And, yes, that includes Ted Bundy and Benjamin Ng.)

Clad in a dark green T-shirt, camouflage pants, gloves, a helmet, and night vision goggles, Bales left the base. According to the government, he walked north along a dirt road for about half a mile and came upon the village of Alikozai, a collection of a dozen mud-and-straw-brick homes. The inhabitants of Alikozai were unimaginably poor, subsisted on migrant farm work, and lived without electricity or indoor plumbing. Many of the homes included multiple families.

Bales entered the home of Haji Sayed Jan and illumined the scene inside with the flashlight at the end of his rifle: women and children. He yelled and ordered the occupants to move into one room. When an elderly woman, Na'ikmarga, resisted, Bales shoved her to the ground and kicked her. A younger woman tried to intervene, and he threw her to the ground and stomped her too. The rest of the women and children ran out of the dwelling, across a courtyard, and into another home.

Bales followed, spotted an old man along the way, and shot him in the head. He then marched five yards across a dirt road and toward the home of Haji Mohamed Naim. A dog in front of the home barked and lunged at Bales, so he shot and killed it. Inside the home Bales encountered a man, woman, and their daughters, ages seven and three. He beat the man as the wife and kids screamed and cried. Bales turned to the crying three-year-old and shot her in the head. He shot the father in the chest and throat. A bullet hit the seven-year-old in the knee.

The surviving occupants, more than two dozen people, mostly women and children, fled to the room of the home's elderly patriarch, Naim, who'd slept through the melee. The children told the old man, "The American is shooting people!" Naim told them to lie low and went to the entryway of the room, where he found Bales. The American raised his rifle and, from less than five feet away, shot the patriarch in the face and neck.

Bales stepped over the old man and entered the room where the women and children recoiled in fear. "We are children," the youngest among them pled in Pashto. "Please don't hurt us!"

He spotted Na'ikmarga, the elderly woman from the previous home, and put a bullet in her head. He began firing into the room, hitting a young boy in both thighs and a girl in the chest and pelvic area. He shot another girl in the back of the head and another boy in the side of the head.

Nearly out of ammo, Bales began the slog back to base.

If that were the end of it, we'd still be talking about the events of that night as one of the greatest atrocities committed by a member of the US military during our occupations of Iraq and Afghanistan. But that was not the end.

No, Sgt. Robert Bales, according to the military, marched back to stock up on more ammunition and weapons. He awoke Staff Sergeant McLaughlin, with whom he'd drank and watched *Man on Fire* a few hours earlier. He told McLaughlin that he'd just killed insurgent combatants (failing to mention that those "insurgents" were in fact unarmed civilians, mostly women, children, and elderly men). McLaughlin was incredulous. Bales said, "Smell my weapon," offering the muzzle of his M4. McLaughlin still couldn't tell whether the rifle had been recently fired. Bales announced that he was going out to do more damage. McLaughlin, still not believing the claims, drifted back to sleep.

Bales added to his arsenal an M320 grenade launcher, 12 grenades, 180 bullets for the M4 rifle, and 15 rounds for the 9-millimeter handgun. This time he headed southeast, along a dirt path the soldiers referred to as No Name Road, toward the village of Naja Bien. There he walked into a home where an impoverished mason named Mohamed Dawud, his wife Masuma, and their six young children, including an infant, slept. The soldier stepped on two of the sleeping children and yanked Dawud out into the courtyard, shouting "Talib! Talib!" Dawud replied, "No Talib. No Talib." Bales then shot Dawud in the head.

Bales reentered the house, grabbed the crying Masuma by the hair, and bashed her head against the wall. He then shoved the muzzle of the 9 millimeter into the infant's mouth and asked Masuma, "Where are the Talib?" He let the infant go but tore the house apart, breaking dishes and furniture, before stepping back out into the courtyard.

He advanced toward the home of Haji Mohamed Wazir, shot the family dog, and stepped inside the house, where there were eleven people, again nearly all women and children, one as young as two years old.

Attempting to defend the occupants in the first room, a thirteen-year-old boy swung a shovel at Bales, striking him in the back. Unfazed, Bales threw the teenager on top of the others. He set his M4 on burst and killed every person in the room, eight in all.

He entered another room, grabbed Wazir's brother and sister-in-law, dragged them into the room with the bodies, and shot them dead as well. Next he took a kerosene can, doused the bodies, lit a match, and set them ablaze. He turned and met Wazir's mother, shot her in the head and chest with the 9 millimeter, and stomped on her head, sending her eyeballs out of their sockets and spraying blood and brains on the wall.

Bales then pulled a decorative rug off the wall and draped it over his shoulders like a cape. Covered in blood, he turned north, toward the base—a killer in a cape traipsing down No Name Road.

Like I said, nothing in my career has been as horrifying as the crimes for which Sergeant Bales was charged. As in the cases of Benjamin Ng and Ted Bundy, however, I believed the accused deserved the best defense possible, that the death penalty the military would no doubt try to impose was an immoral response.

Five days after the massacre, I received a phone call from my office as I drove back from a court appearance in Olympia, Washington. Kari Bales had called my office and said her husband was the accused soldier in the Kandahar killings, though his identity had yet to be made public. She told me her husband had asked for my representation while in a holding cell in Kuwait.

I agreed to meet with her and other family members at a Starbucks near Joint Base Lewis-McChord. The military was taking measures to get Kari and her kids into secure housing on the base because there were threats of retaliation from Islamic fundamentalists. (Hearing that, I immediately thought about my own family's safety if I decided to represent Sergeant Bales.)

Kari pleaded with me to take the case. As usual, I knew it would probably break me financially. Sure, it would mean international attention for my law firm and myself, but I was at the stage of my career where building my résumé or getting national media attention meant little.

I was also concerned about the effect it would have on current and potential clients, who might think I was now too busy to work on their cases. (That fear proved warranted, as my ability to draw new clients was indeed hampered during the Bales case.)

I told Kari I would help "for now," explaining that if the case went down the capital punishment route—very likely—I would need to either bow out or raise at least $2 million. (The average price for a death penalty defense is $3 million to $5 million.) I had about $50,000 in the bank and was paying the salary of five employees and supporting four family members.

A few weeks later my associate Emma Scanlan and I met with Bales at the Fort Leavenworth maximum-security unit in Kansas. The media presence was intense. At times we felt like prisoners in the hotel and actually thought about buying disguises. (Then again, what can a six foot six, long-haired, grey-bearded fellow like me disguise himself as?)

The army had assigned Maj. Tom Hurley as Bales's official military lawyer. The conflict between Hurley and Emma and I was immediate. The rules made the civilian counsel (me) the chief counsel, which irritated Major Hurley. He was arrogant, despite having little experience with cases like this. And when he got defensive and angry—which he did often—his face turned bright red.

He leaked internal e-mails between attorneys to the press—and tried to make it look like Emma and I did it. He got busted a few months into the case and was removed from the team. (A civilian lawyer would have been disbarred for such transgressions.)

We were reassigned a team of wonderful, gifted, experienced JAG lawyers and paralegals. The new team was led by Maj. Greg Malson, assisted by Capt. Aiesi and the talented, dedicated Staff Sgt. Brittany Brinker (my bodyguard in Afghanistan). Major Malson and Emma did the heavy lifting, but we all had supporting roles. And luckily for Sgt. Robert Bales, this new legal team clicked.

As I learned more about the soldier, I realized that, unlike Ng and Bundy, Bales was not a sociopath. Far from it.

To the people in the blue-collar Cincinnati suburb of Norwood, Ohio, population nineteen thousand, where he grew up, he was "Bobby." The youngest of five boys, captain of the high school football team, and the sophomore class president, Bobby was known as a bright, compassionate teenager who went out of his way to befriend Wade, a neighbor boy with developmental disabilities.

Wade's hands were always crossed, his body twitched often, and his face wore a constant, simple smile. He was unable to care for his bodily functions or walk without assistance and always had a towel around his neck for drool collection.

His dad was a single father, so between the ages of twelve and sixteen, Bobby helped take care of Wade. He cleaned up when Wade soiled himself, took Wade to the mall, introduced him to girls, and even took him to the senior prom, where Wade joined Bobby and his girlfriend. Wade is still alive, and his father is forever grateful. Pictures of Sgt. Bales and Wade adorn the walls of Wade's room to this day. (When asked about this during the trial Bales said, "No big deal. I loved Wade." The whole courtroom was in tears, except for the unfeeling military jury.

I asked Bales quietly, "What happened to that Bobby Bales?"

He had tears in his eyes and said, "That Bobby died a long time ago.")

As an adult he was a loving father who enjoyed making chocolate chip pancakes for his son and daughter. He and his wife, Kari, took the kids on camping trips and, recently, on two annual Disney cruises.

I'm not saying Robert Bales is a saint. During a short stint as a stockbroker he was accused of fraud—never proven—and he had once been charged with assault of a woman. And he and his wife were rumored to fight a lot. But he was an exemplary soldier.

In the army, which he joined in the immediate aftermath of 9/11, he had a reputation as a gifted leader. Bales's "superb leadership abilities were essential to the success of the squad and platoon during 100 percent of missions during Operation Iraqi Freedom," wrote a superior in a 2008 evaluation. "Unlimited potential," wrote another. "Select for the most challenging assignments that the Army can offer this outstanding NCO."

He was decorated many times, including in 2007 when the army awarded him the Commendation Medal for "outstanding achievement during the battle of Najaf while serving as a fire team leader." The army said of this honor, "Sgt Bales's heroic actions resulted in mission accomplished. His actions securing a downed helicopter and clearing a trench line resulted in the destruction of a superior numbered enemy."

And yet from almost the moment he was apprehended that night at the gate of VSP Belambay—the rug cape hanging from his shoulders—the military began to paint a completely different image of their man with "unlimited potential." Suddenly he was a sadistic and subpar soldier, one who complained about his superiors, groused over losing promotions, and even openly bemoaned his wife's weight.

The army knew that one of its own had committed an atrocity, and now they wanted as much distance from him as possible. I understood that.

What I didn't understand was how Bobby Bales went from boy-next-door Ohioan and model soldier to mass murderer seemingly overnight.

My office requested his military records. We learned Bales was on his fourth deployment, and the previous three, in Iraq, had been exceptionally tough. He lost part of his foot in 2007 during the Battle of Najaf (the same battle that earned him the Commendation Medal) and suffered a traumatic head injury in 2010 during a vehicle rollover. Add to that the sight of dozens of dead Iraqis, the body parts of which he was sometimes tasked with picking up, and the regular rigors of war—bullets, explosions, the constant high-wire act between life and death. Before his last deployment he was diagnosed with PTSD at Madigan Army Medical Center.

Despite his excellent record, particularly as a leader, he was denied promotion to sergeant first class. Meanwhile he and his wife were on the verge of bankruptcy, soon to lose their home.

The problems escalated during his fourth deployment, which started in February 2012. The atmosphere at VSP Belambay was hostile. The Special Forces soldiers there treated Bales and his fellow soldiers like servants rather than with the respect Special Forces had granted Bales in Iraq. When the elite soldiers did interact with my client, they gave him steroids, alcohol, and other drugs, which further put him on edge.

The challenge for me, Emma, and the JAG defense team was to get a military jury to consider these factors and spare Robert Bales's life. But we had little faith in the military justice system, given our experience with Major Hurley and the fact that our requests to the command were turned down via cursory one-sentence, sometimes one-word, replies. "Request denied" became a constant refrain.

In the military the command (the local general), not a military judge, makes all pretrial decisions. Just one example of the frustration this caused was when the command ordered a sanity board review without any input or notice to us and then denied our request to set some reasonable guidelines. The sanity board was made up of military personnel, mostly doctors, who examined Bales for days without recording the sessions or allowing him access to his legal counsel.

Even more offensive: I received a request, 125 pages, for a security clearance process. Yes, to be a defense lawyer for an accused soldier, you must be vetted *by the opposition*. No way would I participate in such a violation of Bales's Sixth Amendment right to counsel. The first page on the form said it would take approximately two days to fill it out, it had to be filled out while under oath, and all questions needed to be answered. They warned that family members, neighbors, past coworkers, past employers' credit reports, and past travel would be checked out. I could just imagine some low-level government employee knocking on my sister's door and upsetting her. As I said at the time: Want to know of my past issues and problems? Just Google me. My skeletons are not in the closet; they're on the front lawn. This was just another effort at discouraging the use of civilian counsel. I refused, and the issue was dropped. But I wonder how many defense lawyers comply.

I had the added challenge of defending a client accused of crimes committed a world away. When I flew to Kandahar in November 2012, Captain Aiesi, Staff Sergeant Brinker, and I found that interviewing the adult male witnesses was a crash course in cultural diversity. I was instructed never to ask them about their wives. You could ask the men about their health, their kids, their goats—just not *anything* about their wives. In the small courtyard outside the hearing room (remarkable only for its broken cement wall and a lone canary in a cage), a witness with a Taliban tattoo on the top of his hand and I had a calm and seemingly respectful conversation via interpreters. He seemed wise and gentle—until he told me I would be killed for defending Bales. Not *might* be killed but *would.* He was sincere about this threat and oddly polite.

But I fell in love with the children. I wanted to adopt them all. One girl in particular, the most gravely injured of the survivors—presumed dead and found in a pile of bodies—was the sweetest person I've ever met. At one point I went up to her guardian, an uncle maybe, handed him a business card, and told him through the interpreters, "Please tell her if she wants to go to college in the States ever, I will make it happen." I think children in Afghanistan are *born* with PTSD. Unfortunately, they're just used to people having their brains blown out in front of them.

As I mentioned before, during my stay at Camp Nathan Smith sirens blared, warning of incoming rockets, three different times. There were no actual rockets; the Taliban were just fucking with us, though I did break my toe during a mad dash to a bunker at 3:00 AM one morning. And the base was under constant observation by large blimps carrying sophisticated cameras that in a second's notice could be switched to view anything within 360 degrees. I took a photo of one and was told, sternly, by military police never to do that again. (The blimp had apparently caught me taking the photo, and within minutes my transgression had been relayed to the military police.)

My relationship with the troops was odd. To many, mostly enlisted members, I was kind of a hero for helping out a "brother" who had cracked under pressure. I spent many hours smoking cigars in the bunkers with these brave men and women. But to the officers I was a pain in the ass. They knew my job was to blame the army and take the focus off Sergeant Bales. They also knew they could not control me, as I was a civilian, and to them that meant I was a loose cannon.

There was one meaningful exception. I was sitting on the smoking platform with some noncommissioned officers when a colonel joined us. The noncommissioned officers saluted and left. It was just me alone on the platform with this full-bird colonel, who was handsome in a way that reminded me of Clint Eastwood. He offered me a Cuban cigar and said he wanted to share his opinion of Sergeant Bales. He said he had never had a better soldier than Bales in his command and that the "higher-ups" were trying to make Bobby into a rogue soldier rather than take responsibility for the army's mistake of deploying him, knowing he was "broken." He related stories I had already heard about Bales's bravery and dedication. The colonel said he would trust his life in Bales's hands, and had. The war, he said, had put the sergeant over the edge. And the war, he emphasized, was lost. He pointed out the $2 million Stryker vehicles in the distance, unused and covered in tarps. He said the US military should "blow them up" and go home, because our presence in the country was doing no one any good. He felt guilty that he couldn't help Bales but said he had been "instructed" not to. We finished our cigars, and he left me on the smoking platform.

It was around this time that I began to fully comprehend the toll a hopeless war had on these brave men and women. I could see it in their faces. There was a resignation, a distant look—a look I have seen in dispirited people my whole life.

On paper the military code of justice is very logical and fair; in practice, for Bales, the fix was in. No way would the army take responsibility for Bobby Bales's meltdown, even though the government did pay over $900,000 in cash to victims' families within two days of the incident. We knew the army wanted to avoid the true facts of Bales's mental health and the politics and dysfunction at the FOB where he was stationed. We hired the best mental health experts and knew they would produce extensive, factual reports. As these reports trickled in, we approached the army prosecutors with the idea of taking the death penalty off the table.

The chief prosecutor, Jay Morse, was recently promoted to colonel. He and Judge Jeffery Nance would exchange e-mails addressing each other as "Dear Jay" or "Dear Jeff," without even the slightest attempt at formality. We, the civilian lawyers, were "Mr. Browne" and "Ms. Scanlan." It was clear the prosecution and the judge had their marching orders. Early on we had a formal meeting with the general in charge of Joint Base Lewis-McChord in an effort to stop him referring to the case as a capital case. During our PowerPoint presentation it was clear nobody was listening. You know that look: people staring right at you but who you know are not paying attention. Of course, it was easy to understand the lack of interest, as the facts were so gruesome and it was an international political case.

Finally, Secretary of Defense Leon Panetta made public comments suggesting that the death penalty was on the table. This is usually a big no-no, since it could be seen as undue command influence.

How to deal with this stacked deck?

Our play was to show we could prove the army and Special Forces caused the massacre. We told the prosecutors that the whole world would know the army's dirty little secrets: the payoffs to the victims' families, the pressure on the rank and file to not cooperate with the defense, the dysfunction at the forward operating base, and how Special Forces encouraged Bales's drug and alcohol use. We would also establish that the army failed to treat Bales after knowing he had mental health issues. We would, on a worldwide stage, put the army and its leadership on trial. That we had gotten nowhere after spending over $5 trillion on the war effort. That while we send guns, rockets, and drones to Afghanistan, the Chinese are building hospitals there, making them far more likely to win the hearts and minds of the people.

We had the facts to back all this up, and the army knew it. So they agreed to a plea bargain. We wanted the death penalty off the table at any cost because we knew if it was an option, a military jury chosen by a general would impose the ultimate penalty. We had little hope we would succeed.

But we did.

The army said we had to agree that Bobby was a rogue solider. OK, so we had to agree he went out and killed women and children because he had money problems, because he had voluntarily taken steroids and alcohol, and—most appallingly—because his wife was heavyset. "OK," we said, "whatever. Just take the death penalty option away." And they did.

In June 2013 we had a trial to determine whether Bales would receive a life sentence with or without parole. (Life with parole carried a twenty-year minimum.) But once again the deck was stacked and the outcome inevitable and fixed. The general who'd wanted the death penalty imposed selected the jury panel. I will never forget the stone-cold looks on the jurors' faces during the whole trial—as if I was pleading with Mount Rushmore. We decided not to put on a mental health defense, as it would just allow the government to put hack psychologists on the stand who would, without examining Bales, say he was a self-centered sociopath and a bad solider. Instead we concentrated on Sergeant Bales as a person before and after his four deployments.

The jury, however, knew what was expected of them, and nothing would have changed the outcome. They imposed life without parole.

What do I think happened in Kandahar Province on May 11, 2012? I think a good soldier with PTSD and steroids in his veins drank whiskey and shouldn't have. I think the toll of four deployments was too much. I think a movie about a revenge fantasy got mixed up in his brain, so by the time he was around actual innocent children—like the fictional one avenged in the film—he got it all wrong.

I think Staff Sgt. Robert Bales snapped.

And as I've said, I think we are the cause. You can't engage in two wars—one of which, Iraq, was completely unjustified—send hundreds of thousands of young men into the maw of battle over and over again, and expect nothing bad to come of it.

I thought about this when I was in Kandahar—especially every time that siren blared late at night and I had forty-seven seconds to run barefoot over sharp rocks to the cement bunker, not knowing whether or not I was gasping my last breath. I felt jarred and perpetually on edge, and I knew I was only in it for a week, with no one aiming weapons at me. I couldn't imagine what it would be like knowing thousands of people were out to kill me for months on end, deployment after deployment.

I can only hope that some courageous leader in the future will see how the system failed Sergeant Bales—who had put his life on the line through four tours in two hellish wars defending the freedoms no longer provided him—and commute his sentence. After all, Lt. William Calley in the Vietnam War was responsible for killing more than one hundred people, mostly women and children, during the My Lai massacre, and his sentence was ultimately commuted, which showed at least that the government had taken some responsibility. I don't see that as an option with our present leaders, who ignore the war and its costs in dollars and human suffering. For now, the lesson I've taken away from all this is beware those who gain their power by withholding their compassion.

By week's end, after we had conducted our interviews in Kandahar and I climbed aboard a helicopter and it arced over a desiccated, war-pocked land—toward the airfield where the rickety 727 awaited—I wondered how long it would be before we saw the real toll of these wars. I wondered if we'd ever truly comprehend the cost.

And I wondered how many more Robert Baleses we have created.

EPILOGUE

People often ask if I think Ted Bundy killed Deborah Beeler. The short answer is no. Aside from a few coincidences—both she and her manner of death fit the Bundy profile—there is no direct evidence that Ted was active in the Bay Area in early 1970.

But the question itself brings up all kinds of complicated thoughts. I've never been able to shake the knowledge that Ted knew about my loss before he sought me out as his counsel—and that he kept that secret from me for years. More complicated still is the fact that I defended Ted knowing he had killed countless women just like Debbie.

It was the ultimate test: How committed was I to this life of defending the rights and lives of others, even the most heinous, no matter how much their crimes personally impact me?

I believe I made the right choice. But drawing up those memories has brought back the dark side of his life and mine.

You know that vague sense you sometimes experience when something is wrong but you don't quite know what it is because it's not fully formed? Like the start of an illness. Awake or asleep, there it is. This feeling has been with me, off and on, since Ted's execution. The best I can do is force it into messy, possibly unanswerable questions.

Does helping the devil make you a devil too? That is, while defending Ted Bundy did I somehow absorb evil? And shame, shame ups the ante with an insidious hiss: Is there something wrong with me that somehow makes it possible for me to defend evil?

For so long I felt responsible for the lives Ted took. I was the one who assisted him in winning special privileges at the Glenwood Springs jail. I told him about the death penalty laws in Florida, where he fled after his second escape, and I was the first person he called from Lake City while he was still basically at large and unknown to the authorities there.

I have never confessed this before, but I sometimes think I should have killed Ted in his Aspen cell after his first escape. I was never searched when I entered the building. I could have easily smuggled in a gun. I had known that if he was ever free again, it was inevitable that he would brutally take the lives of more innocents. But that would have answered my question right there, wouldn't it?

Killing Ted would have made me more like Ted.

I was once questioned on an afternoon talk show, "What differentiates people like Ted Bundy from the rest of us?"

My response was spontaneous: "He lacked any notion that we are all somehow connected."

My law partner at the time referred to the answer as more of John Henry's "woo woo shit." But the thing is, I have had deep feelings of "oneness" in my life.

My first sense of the sacred connection among all things happened as a child in the desert of New Mexico, and I've experienced this deep knowledge of connectedness maybe ten times since. I saw and felt it during the 9/11 tragedies. Many people focus on the horrible images of the planes hitting the towers. I remember how there was a oneness that transcended the external drama. I will never forget a TV image of a well-dressed man with a Rolex on his bloody arm working with a down-and-out street person to help a mortally wounded woman to safety. That is oneness at its best. The reality was the sameness, not the differences.

"How can you defend these people?"

The armored defense lawyer will deliver a practiced reply: "Because the Constitution requires it." The deeper, meaningful inquiry gets brushed aside, but the truth for me is it's a matter of survival.

Experiencing the unsheltered reality of life and death makes me feel alive. When we think of experiencing a spiritual *Aha!*, we conjure images of pristine beaches, rugged mountaintops, or monastic seclusion. For me they are just as likely to arise in a smelly prison cell or on a bug-infested mattress in a tiny compound in Afghanistan. I may not be well understood when I say that, in a way, crime scenes are sacred places. I have always approached them in this way. Autopsy photos are personal, real, graphic, and powerful. I have no choice but to feel deep respect, both for the dead and the victims, guilty or not, of the system.

I am not a burning bush sort of guy. I don't have profound moments on a daily basis. Mine is a real struggle to deepen my life in the face of many obstacles—to search for meaning in the midst of representing mass murderers. My friends and associates have a hard time reconciling my private spiritual quest with my public image as an arrogant pit bull defense lawyer. (A frustrated prosecutor actually once called me a "pit bull on crack.") But being spiritual in my world is not as difficult as dealing with judges and prosecutors who don't see the world the way I do. My relationship with them is a challenge: I want to be condescending, forceful, and rude, but that's my ego not my spirit. I force myself to see them as people like me—flawed but trying their best—and try to remind them of their power to practice compassion as well as punishment. I once quoted Buddha to a small-town judge, and he said to me, "Bubba? Bubba who?" (I have also quoted Bob Dylan, Jimi Hendrix, Friedrich Nietzsche, Carl Jung, and Doonesbury in briefs, with mixed reactions.)

The combination of insecurity and arrogance has served me well as a trial lawyer. I'm convinced that when I am at my best in the courtroom, some big voice in the back of the room will shout out, "You're just a fake, and you know it!" This fear supports the reason all gifted trial lawyers win: we are insecure, and we overprepare. I have driven many associates and staff away by my need to know more than anybody else about the case. This approach confuses and exasperates my opponents, judges, and the public.

And so I give lots of talks and speeches to organizations at conferences and other gatherings but rarely get invited back. The reason, I realize, is my directness and weird sense of humor. I once gave a talk with a prosecutor at a high school assembly of three hundred or more students. The prosecutor told them that the reason he was a district attorney was because of his time in "Nam" and the blight of drugs in America. I followed his speech by telling the students that the reason I was a lawyer was because I was arrested, wrongfully, and there was a difference between drug use and drug abuse. The reaction was immediate. The principal said, "Time is up," and later wrote me a nasty letter.

This was similar to the reaction of the Washington State Bar Association when I spoke at a convention (with a thousand or more in attendance) and stated that the ethical rules are "advisory" rather than "mandatory." The speech got good reviews, but the mucky-mucks at the bar were offended. I was never invited back. I continue to this day to be in conflict with the bar association. My impression is it is an organization of good ole boys protecting the status quo. You rarely, if ever, see a prosecutor or big-firm lawyer sanctioned by this group of elites.

But if I'm being honest, my belief in the interconnectedness of us all—again, the thing I believe Ted Bundy lacked—is what has made the seemingly impossible possible. My accomplishments required the help of many others and often divine intervention, which continues to make me wonder at the magic in life.

No one thought I could save the life of a young man who shot and killed thirteen people. But I did. The prospect of getting a plea bargain, with four states, to save Ted Bundy from the death penalty was slim to none, but I did (even if he didn't ultimately take the deal). Bringing exposure to the corruption of an entire criminal justice system and the corruption of a community seemed a daunting task, but with the help of others I began to unravel the nightmarish reality known as the Wenatchee Witch Hunt, leading to the exoneration of more than thirty wrongfully accused people.

Recently, with Colton Harris-Moore, I was told it was impossible for nearly seventy criminal cases from two different countries, six different states, the federal government, and many counties in Washington State to be consolidated into two cases and result in concurrently reasonable sentences, but I accomplished that task.

And, finally, no one thought I could spare the life of Sgt. Robert Bales. But that happened too.

My fervor has increased over the years as I've tried to make sense of our acceptance of unjustified wars fought by the poor for the upper class, of the very government that could allow my father and others to create a device powerful enough to end humankind, of witnessing people beaten by cops, of spending several nights in jail alongside others who were not just oppressed by the system but also utterly destroyed by it.

While I can't say I've changed the world, I can say it certainly has changed me. And I do know that I've made a significant difference in many lives, one case at a time. For me that is enough.

APPENDIX A

JOHN HENRY BROWNE'S TEN RULES FOR TRIALS

1. Know your case from both sides.
2. Never waive opening statements.
3. No boilerplate.
4. Tell a story. A trial is a drama.
5. Don't lie to a jury or make promises you can't keep.
6. Try all cases you can win. Only plea bargain because you can't win.
7. Always hide the ball from the prosecution.
8. Don't fight issues that don't matter.
9. Always consider resting without putting on a case.
10. Complex preparation. Simple presentation.

APPENDIX A

APPENDIX B
THE LETTERS OF TED BUNDY

October 31, 1976

Dear John:
Thank you for your letter of October 27. I too, wish the circumstances of our first contact since last February were different. I had intended to write to you on several occasions during the past several months to express my appreciation for the moral and professional support you have given me and my girlfriend and others close to me.

Recent developments seem to indicate that I will be desperately in need of such support in the near future. I have had a tendency to be overly analytical about the motivations of the Colorado authorities in filing their case at this time. I suppose my real concern should not be "why" they filed but "what," they filed. Whatever their reasoning, they have taken the plunge and are now committed to follow through. However, according to their own admission, their affidavit outlines the same case they had eight months ago. It is safe to say that bringing the case at this time was prompted by considerations other than the circumstantial evidence contained in the arrest warrant affidavit.

Whether or not their case is a strong one, and I am convinced it is not, the threat I face is considerable for numerous non-evidentiary reasons. First and foremost is the publicity. Next comes my conviction for kidnapping in Utah. The third strike against me involves the significant potential for official misconduct (i.e., falsifying evidence) on the part of those who, "believe," in my guilt and feel as it is their duty to bring about my conviction.

Finally, I am at an extreme disadvantage due to both a lack of funds to hire attorneys, investigators and experts, and to the prosecutors' seemingly unlimited investigative resources; resources which can, quote, "create" an image of credibility when no case exists. It is this last point [that] most concerns me. If I could fight them on an equal footing, I have no doubt I would be acquitted. One man, an attorney, [name removed], no matter how skilled or competent, is no match to prepare a defense to equal the complex case the prosecution has created. Without more assistance, the consequences to my life could be fatal.

You have no obligation to come to my aid, but I am begging you to do so because my life hangs in the balance. I am asking you to provide whatever services you can offer, because I am immensely impressed by your legal intelligence and more so because I like you and feel comfortable with you. I need

your help now more than I have ever needed help before in my life. What more can I say except "please" help me?
Sincerely,
Ted
PS: I will avoid discussing details of the Colorado case in letters. I will only talk about the case directly to my present attorneys. If you should have questions, submit them through my present attorneys, and if you haven't read Colorado's affidavit, I will ask my present attorney to send you a copy, should you be in a position to help, that is.

November 1976

Dear John:
I received your letter of November 10 today and find some encouragement in your news, if only because it indicates your continuing willingness to help. I would like to keep my options open regarding my final choice of counsel. I have had no contact with my present attorney and will be unable to make a decision about him until I have talked to him personally and at length. I hope you will understand my reservations as it is my belief that I must have complete confidence in someone in whose hands my life will be placed. I have written my present attorney asking his opinion on several critical matters, including extradition, and requesting a meeting with him before I go to Colorado.

Of course I would prefer an alliance between my present attorney and you. If I had a choice at this moment between the two of you, I would choose you, but I am not sure I can afford that choice.

I am in complete agreement concerning guaranteed reimbursement for expenses and lost salary should I ask you to handle my case. Is there any way you could give me some general estimate of what this might amount to for Ressler and you? I know how difficult this would be, but if I had an idea, I would be able to determine whether or not I am capable of raising such an amount at all.

I wouldn't hold you to an estimate in any event, but if you are out of the ballpark, I had better know now.

The question of extradition carries more significance for me than whether by fighting it I can avoid it. I will be extradited too no matter what, but by opposing extradition, are there advantages which outweigh the disadvantages?

In your opinion, in a habeas corpus hearing on the matter, would not it be possible to expose more of the prosecution's case, if indeed there is more, as well as, quote, "freeze" what they already have? I think there is a positive potential here.

Second, I am convinced that much time will be required to prepare my defense. The prosecution has been investigating and building their case for 14 months. God knows how many man-hours and how much money has been expended. Positions, such as admitting evidence as a, quote, "common scheme and plan," involving incidents in other jurisdictions have been thoroughly briefed. I need time, and I would rather spend it in the Utah State Prison than in the Pitkin County Jail, fighting extradition. Fighting extradition will buy some time, don't you think?

The negative consequences to such a fight would be, as you observed, publicity and inferring my uncooperativeness. This is a difficult issue, which ultimately involves the whole area of pretrial publicity in my case.

The first question is what is the volume and substance of publicity at this point in the Glenwood Springs/Aspen area, and what is it likely to be in the future?

I will ask my attorney to make a study of this, should a motion for postponement on grounds of pretrial publicity be warranted. Will my opposition to extradition do any further harm? I am not convinced that it will, especially since I intend to make clear the reasons why I am fighting extradition: 1) I was not in Colorado at the time of the commission of the crime; and 2) Need time to overcome great prosecution advantage.

Bad reasons, you know, I just thought the effect of fighting extradition is not nearly as damaging as the impact of losing that fight, which will eventually happen.

Now I have changed my mind a lot, damn it. I think it is perfectly suicidal to rush into a strange state and be represented by an unknown attorney who has but a few weeks to prepare against a case, which the prosecution has been plotting for over a year. I believe it is literally suicide. What do you recommend?

This is a case which will be won or lost on the ability of the defense to do the following: 1) Thoroughly field investigate; and 2) Suppress testimony related to other crimes.

I will elaborate more on that issue later. Can't fit any more paper into this envelope. Thanks again for the letter.

Hang in there,

Ted

November 29, 1976

Dear John,

My issue of the Wednesday, November 24, 1976, Seattle Times contains an article on A4 with a bold heading, quote: "FBI Links Hair Samples to Bundy." This is just not something I expected from the Times. What are they doing, warming up the cross for my crucifixion?

This is one of the most flagrant examples of prosecution by the press that I have seen. The worst thing about this Seattle Times article is that it will be carried by the wire services and broadcast in the Denver and the Aspen area.

Damn it, John, I can't get used to this abuse. The impact of the article is deadly, without the knowledge that hair samples are far from being identification.

He goes on to mention, quote, "several" eyewitnesses, when, as you may know, there was one woman who picks my picture one year after the Colorado disappearance and stated that she had passed a, quote, "strange" man in the hall the night of the disappearance, who looked like me, an observation she neglected to mention to police until a year later.

Note also how the fallacious escape materials—also how the escape material allegation is injected to magnify the inferences of guilt.

The intent of the article is purely malicious and prejudicial. I feel powerless as I watch my conviction firsthand by the media. I see this article as part of a calculated attempt to convince the public of the official belief in my guilt, and to influence the outcome of the Colorado trial.

I had to do something. Enclosed you will find a letter to the editor of the Times. Would you read it and if it seems appropriate, do what you can to have it published? "Thanks."
Best regards,
Ted

July 7, 1977

Dear John:
Good heavens . . . it has been over three weeks since my early morning call to you upon my return to captivity, and I am just getting around to saying, quote, "thank you," to you for coming to my aid, coming to Aspen, and just generally making me feel less like a fumbling, stupid idiot I was behaving like.

Aw, but that adventurous chapter is behind me, or so I would like to think at this moment. The ghosts of my escapade will return [in] the form of five counts and a new information. I will behave like the hardened convict I am and say, quote, "Fuck it. I have got broad shoulders." That is what a hard con would say, isn't it?

Since my return, I have been in procrastination—in a procrastination inspired slump. ("I have got plenty of time; the suppression hearing isn't for two months.")

Instead of working, I have been doing push-ups, pull-ups, jumping rope, and have done my best to emulate Tarzan. I am eating nuts, took vitamins, gagged on nutritional yeast, and in the process have (at least to my own mind) become a superb physical specimen.

Now I am sitting here wondering what makes me want to be so damned healthy.

Today I emerged from both my, "slump," and my Fourth of July depression, and decided to entertain myself with the criminal law again. What a shameful attitude. However, working on the case has become both fun and distracting, an attitude which no doubt reinforces the point of view that I shouldn't be handling this case—but Christ, if a person can't enjoy the work, why do it? It is just plain challenging.

It is also just a bit frightening at times, too.

Today, for instance, I decided to research the area of suppression of evidence material and favorable to the defense. Since several re-readings of the documents in question convinced me that they alone might warrant a new trial.

I took the amicus brief that you wrote in the Wright case. I looked up a few cases, the most recent US Supreme Court being United States v. Aggers. What a horrendous case. The Berger Court is very unsound. Agurs [*sic*], on top of Brady, is like mustard on top of chocolate cake. It just doesn't make sense and gave me indigestion. Until . . . I talked to an attorney (I knew they were good for something); the attorney just happened to mention that Aggers came down in June 1976 and that all of the discovery in my case took place between November 1975 and February 1976. Thus Brady and its progeny, free of the Aggers sliding rule (this is where the prosecutor slides everything into the police files and says he never saw the stuff, honest!) would be applied in my case.

Still, this is no guarantee, but I am more confident about receiving a new trial now than ever before.

At this point, however, I think I would lose a new trial in the kidnapping case, but hell, getting there would be half the fun, anyway. So I am fat and healthy, munching on something called, "peanuts and caramel log," one of many goodies sent to me by my friends. Sounds disgusting, and it is, but I have a munchy mentality and I truly love it.

Thanks again. You have done a great deal for me. I want you to know how I recognize it and appreciate it. Now try to take that to the bank. How much is it worth to you to have me tell you that I can't imagine a finer defense attorney than yourself? It's true. I consider myself an expert on the good ones and the bad ones.

Best wishes,
Ted

June 1, 1979

Dear John:
During the time you stayed in Tallahassee, we had a chance to discuss at length developments in the case. If you feel anything like I do, you are sick and tired of hearing about the Bundy case.

It was great seeing you and talking with you again. There can be little question as to why you are doing so well in your practice; you are an exceptionally bright and concerned person. You are much more than that, but the way in which you reach out to those whose causes you advocate is extraordinary.

I am fortunate to have had you on my side and there is no adequate manner to express my gratitude for the time and expense you took to come help me, except to give you a deeply felt, quote, "thank you," in every way.

Best regards,
Ted

October 15, 1984

Dear John,

Are you still there? I mean, are you still in the Smith Tower? I hope this is forwarded to you if you are not.

How are you? Still running? It has been a while since we have been in touch. Carole told me that she and our daughter, Rosebud, just paid a visit to you around Christmas time last year.

I have a favor to ask of you. Would you mind taking the enclosed letter I have written to someone associated with the Green River Task Force who has some sense and can be trusted to take the right steps to see that the letter both receives proper consideration and remains confidential?

I know firsthand how professional egos and agency rivalries and conventional police close-mindedness can drastically reduce the effectiveness of an organization like the Task Force.

I am pretty sure I can provide them with some valuable information if we can transcend such limitations. So please give it to someone with an open mind and a creative outlook on investigating such cases. Does such an animal exist? On October 1, I wrote a letter to the Task Force, which I sent via a superior court judge in Tacoma, a long time family friend. I asked him to let me know that he had received and forwarded it, but in two weeks I have heard nothing from him or the task force.

Actually, I would have sent the letter through you in the first place, but it just didn't occur to me until after I mailed the letter.

So what do you think of the Task Force? What do you know about it? Is it chasing its tail? Is it disorganized? Does it have competent people? Is it well run? Would the people there resent or reject out-of-hand my offer of information and assistance?

There are a number of reasons why I offer my help to the Task Force at this time (please go ahead and read the letter I have written to them, by the way, and it may give you a better understanding of what I am doing.) Basically, though, the case fascinates me and challenges me. I would like to figure out what makes the Green River guy tick, and I figure I have as good a chance of doing that as anyone on the Task Force. And I also think that the time seems right in some inexplicable sort of way, and I find myself saying, quote, "Why not put some of your knowledge and unique perspective to use. It could be interesting."

I don't fancy myself playing detective, but I will bet I can play the man or men they are looking for better than any of them.

Please let me know you received this and what, if anything, happened when you passed it along.

Thank you for your help. Take care of yourself.

Peace.

Ted

P.S. And remember, you can arrange to reach me by phone, if you wish.

October 15, 1984

Dear Task Force Members,

On October 1, 1984, I wrote a letter to you and sent it via a superior court judge in Tacoma. I asked the judge to give me some kind of indication that he would—he had received and forwarded that letter to you.

During the intervening two weeks, I have heard nothing from the judge or you. I don't know what the problem is, or even if there is a problem, but I thought I had better try another means of contacting you in case, for whatever reason, the first failed.

Therefore, I send this letter through John Henry Browne, a Seattle criminal defense attorney, who I know and trust.

I must admit that I am being cautious in approaching you. It would not look good to my fellow prisoners if it became known that I offered to help and provide information for your investigation.

This is one reason I do not want to let it be known that I am writing you.

Mail passes through many hands before it leaves this place, and there are too many curious minds for me to address a letter to you directly.

A broader concern of mine is that my offer of information and whatever other assistance you determine I can provide not be made known outside the Task Force, especially not to the news media, in part because of the reason I stated above, and in part because such publicity could hamper your investigation in some way.

Okay, with that in mind, I will tell you, as I told you in my other letter, that I have information which I believe would be useful to your investigation. I have a unique perspective on the Green River case, which, while I may not provide you with anything you haven't thought of before, may cause you to refocus and read re-examine [*sic*] things you may have neglected or dismissed for some reason or another.

Let me explain how I came to realize I had something of value to offer you at this late date.

While I gather that the Green River matter has been a source of concern in the Pacific Northwest for a couple of years or so, news of these murders did not begin to filter down to this far corner of the country until maybe a year ago, as far as I can recall. Even then, news accounts here were infrequent and very brief. I am sure the news coverage here was microscopic compared to what has been seen in the Seattle Tacoma area.

Not having access to regular, detailed, and comprehensive news coverage, I did not have an opportunity to gain any kind of feel for the Green River situation. I had no basis for developing any ideas or insights. I had no reason to go out of my way to learn more about the cases. There were other things on my mind.

Then 2 to 3 months ago, I began receiving a local newspaper from Tacoma. It was the first time in over five years I have received a daily newspaper from the Northwest. It was about a month ago that I got my first real taste of the local coverage of the Green River investigation when the body of a woman, believed to be linked to the Green River cases, was discovered in a remote area of Pierce County.

The news coverage of that discovery, and subsequent and related articles were something of a revelation. I got a feel for what was happening, albeit tentative, and was based on pitifully few facts. But I know your man in a way that facts alone cannot accomplish.

I do not know his face, but I have some pretty good ideas on where you can look to see him for yourselves. There are many reasons why I want to see if I can be of some help to you. I won't claim some noble, civic-minded motivation. Basically, the case has really begun to intrigue me. But I am sure it intrigues lots of people. The difference is I have knowledge and a point of view to add to your case investigation like no one else does.

I may simply have reached the point where I realized I have something of value and the chance to use it productively.

I would like your assurance that this letter, and any other communications we may have, will be kept strictly confidential and that no one outside the Task Force will be made aware of what I have said here or will say should we enter into a dialogue.

If you wish to communicate with me by mail, please do so by sending a letter through a prosecutor, lawyer or a judge that is clearly marked, "legal mail." Such mail is opened in my presence and not read. Other mail is opened in the mailroom and may be read.

If you would rather send someone to talk with me, I would welcome the opportunity. Eventually, I think you stand to gain more if you meet with me personally. If you do decide to send someone to Florida, I suggest that you have someone from a local office of the FBI help you gain entrance to the prison without divulging the exact reason for your visit.

Well, there you have it. I have no way of knowing if you need or want anything I have to offer. All I can do is let you know I am willing to help any way I can. The rest is up to you.

Good luck.

Sincerely,
Ted Bundy

ACKNOWLEDGMENTS

I began writing this memoir seven years ago on the too-few vacations I spent at my house in Mexico. I'd bring my first-generation Apple laptop—which I still use—along with boxes of notes, letters, photos, and newspaper articles. After five years of struggling to write about my experiences with Ted Bundy, my recollections seemed finished, at least as far as I was concerned, since I never imagined my story would be published. But after a few new high-profile cases and after word got out that I'd been working on a memoir, CBS News producers Paul LaRosa and Susan "Z" Zirinsky and *48 Hours* host Peter Van Sant expressed great interest, and these very kind and busy people took time to read my story. Peter and Z agreed to support and promote the memoir, but not until it was better organized and written.

Then the real blessing: James Ross Gardner, now editor in chief of *Seattle Met* magazine. James had written a profile of me for *Seattle Met* ("The Law and John Henry !*@#ing Browne") and later agreed to help with the manuscript. Well help he did. If there is any literary value to this book, it's James's doing. He put months into making this interesting and readable. He is a true craftsman, and a better friend would be hard to imagine. Thanks again, JRG.

Z introduced me to agent Frank Weimann, and he and I hit it off. A man of few words but great wisdom, Frank truly believed in the project. Fate and Frank worked in tandem when the latter struck a contract with Chicago Review Press, and our team was blessed with the addition of editor Yuval Taylor. I was warned that editors were brutal, frank, and demanding. True, but Yuval was always supportive, and the finished book is much better because of him.

Lance Rosen is a well-respected entertainment lawyer whose early encouragement for this project was seemingly limitless. He has taught me so much, mostly how to listen. He's now one of my best friends, and we continue to deepen that friendship as we explore possible spin-off projects.

Others in the literary and entertainment field who provided support and important criticism include Kany Levine, the late Ann Rule, Jeff Benedict, Kristin Hanna, and Dustin Lance Black.

My long, strange trip began, of course, with my birth family, all now deceased but never dead to me. My mother, Helen, beautiful inside and out, always told me I could be successful at whatever my path was—as long as I stayed on the path. She was unconditional love embodied. My sister, Bonnie, who struggled through life with mental illness, loved me deeply and had a laugh that shook the roof. We moved around so much as children that we were by default each other's best friends. My niece Stephanie Kirkland and her two kids were there for me when my parents and sister we very ill. And of course my father, Harry, a very complicated man who only learned late in life it was not a weakness to show your love, was wise beyond belief and supportive of me—even though he always wanted me to live an easier life. I miss him every day.

The true gifts in my life, my sons Eli and Matt, taught me the most important lesson of all, patience. I am so proud that both are often referred to as the kindest young men imaginable. I never planned on being a dad, but what a gift it has been. I love them dearly.

Most recently there's my own, true "hard-headed woman," whose own ostensible contradictions—she's a former Ralph Lauren model who can skin a deer—has helped me understand mine and turn my nagging insecurities into minor issues. And for that I'm ever grateful.

Special thanks and gratitude for my lost loves, Deborah Beeler, Ann "Punky" Babson, and the entire Audrey Hillman family. They all offered so much, even when I gave back too little.

Thank you to the loving friends who changed my life forever. My true soul mate was Keith Hansen, and I'm grateful to his wife Susan and their kids Mike and Kati. After Keith passed, his cousin John took his place as my best friend, and then he too passed. My teacher Richard Moss taught me about the sacred nature of life, and I met many friends on that path, particularly Barbara "Beau" Taylor—a more beautiful soul you will never meet. Sylvia Mathews and I were on the same path for years, and she saved my life more than once. Richard Miller, the caretaker of a sacred place, Wilber Hot Springs, also introduced me to the beauty of sobriety. I'm also grateful to the late Betty Ford for obvious reasons. Dan Crystal started as my shrink and remains my shrink and a true friend. Thank you forever to my fellow travelers in the Crystal Palace Guard: Chris, Michael, Willie, Buz, and Jeff.

Others have have stuck with me through many ups and downs, always with love and care, especially Lorie Hutt and her husband, Rick. I just don't know what negative path I would have gone down without Lorie, my office manager and life manager. She is, simply put, a saint. Thanks also to Allen Ressler, and to former and current members of my staff: Emma Scanlan, Colleen Hartl, Michael Lee, and Susan Gilpen. I get the credit; they do the work.

I'm indebted to my teachers of the law: Warren Wolfson and his wife Joanne, Sherman Magidson, Skip Andrew, and my first and only true boss, Don Horowitz.

I would not have stuck with the law without the inspiration and courage of many judges and even prosecutors who practiced compassion as well as punishment: Judges John C. Coughenour, William Downing, Robert Lasnik, Ricardo Martinez, Jeffrey Miller, Marsha Pechman, C. Z. Smith, and my beloved William O. Douglas (who I was proud to know); and prosecutors Jeff Baird, Hugh Barber, Tim Bradshaw, Vince Lombardi (grandson of the famous football coach), Norm Maleng, Dan Satterberg, Frank Jenny, and Sarah Vogel.

Finally, I am grateful for the inspiration of Leonard Cohen, John Lennon, Rumi, Ram Dass, Van Morrison, Bruce Cockburn, and others who have filled my life with music, metaphysics, and beauty. You too, Uncle Pat.

INDEX